HEARTWARMING

♥

PLASTIC CANVAS™

The Needlecraft Shop™

PUBLISHER / Donna Robertson
DESIGN DIRECTOR / Fran Rohus
PRODUCTION DIRECTOR / Ange Van Arman

EDITORIAL
Senior Editor / Janet Tipton
Editorial & Graphics Team / Kristine Kirst,
Trina Burch, Marianne Telesca, Kim Pierce, Jeanne Austin

PHOTOGRAPHY
Photographers / Mary Craft, Tammy Cromer-Campbell
Photo Stylist & Coordinator / Ruth Whitaker

PRODUCTION
Book Design & Layout / Debby Keel
Production Team / Danny Martin, Minette Smith

PRODUCT DESIGN
Design Coordinator / Brenda Wendling

BUSINESS
C.E.O. / John Robinson
Vice President / Customer Service / Karen Pierce
Vice President / Marketing / Greg Deily
Vice President / M.I.S. / John Trotter

CREDITS
Sincerest thanks to all the designers, manufacturers and professionals whose dedication
has made this book possible. Special thanks to David Norris of
Quebecor Printing Book Group, Kingsport, TN.

Library of Congress Cataloging-in-Publication Data
ISBN: 1-57367-078-2
First Printing: 1996
Library of Congress Catalogue Number: 96-71903
Published and Distributed by *The Needlecraft Shop, LLC.*,
Big Sandy, Texas 75755
Printed in the United States of America

Dear Friends,

Grandma and Grandpa lived right behind us when I was growing up. I remember many an evening watching Granny crochet and mend, seated in her comfy upholstered rocker, her needlework illuminated by light coming from an old floor lamp. Beside her chair was a small hardwood chest of drawers. I loved rummaging around in those drawers — they were filled with things like brightly colored bias seam binding and threads, stretchy elastic and a variety of needles and thimbles.

My favorite drawer in her sewing chest was full of buttons — a rainbow of colors in slightly different shapes and sizes … I recall wondering if I would ever be able to sew like Mom and Granny.

One day when I was in third grade, a button fell off one of my favorite school dresses. That afternoon Mom told me I was old enough to sew the button on myself. Though I had watched her and Granny sew and hand-hem countless dresses for my sister and me over the years, it was an exciting and awkward moment when my small fingers first reached for needle and thread. Threading the needle was a real challenge, but Mom patiently sat with me and encouraged my efforts until I had mastered the skill adequately enough to move on to the next lesson: knotting the end of the thread.

My knots were bulky at first, but at least the thread didn't pull completely through the fabric. When Mom showed me how to hold the button between my left thumb against the top of the fabric and my finger against the bottom of the fabric, I felt just like I did when trying to balance myself for the first time on a bicycle! Then came the challenge of holding the button and fabric together in one hand and actually sewing with my right hand … I had my fill of needle piercings at an early age.

It took many tries before I could swiftly sew on a button and also have it properly aligned with the buttonhole. Nowadays, with zippers and other closures on many clothing items, buttons are more decorative than essential.

Today my stitching bag has a permanent spot beside my favorite chair and my buttons are kept in an old cookie tin. Even though my eighteen-year-old daughter thinks that stitchery is mostly for grannies, I've found her in my chair on occasion, sewing buttons on her favorite shirts. Someday I hope to have a granddaughter. I want to let her look inside that tin and touch all the buttons and feel, like I felt, the magic pull of needle and thread.

Maybe she can start younger and without so much bloodshed, using tools of plastic canvas stitchery: sturdy plastic canvas instead of easy-to-soil fabric, fuzzy yarn instead of microscopic thread and a nice blunt tapestry needle … projects and tools may change over time, but the pleasures of stitching will always warm the heart.

Janet

Table of Contents

Country Jamboree

Baby Hugs

Springtime Fresh

Household Classics

Awesome Autumn

Christmas Cheer

Fun & Games

Country Jamboree

Spend the afternoon
with Grandma putting the
final touches on your entry
for the blue ribbon needlework contest. Enjoy a taste
of her award-winning
blackberry pie fresh from the
oven, as its fragrance slowly
wafts by from the kitchen.
Now, with your project
finished just in time,
gather your herd and
head to the county fair!

Slim Snowman

Designed by Michele Wilcox

LEVEL OF DIFFICULTY: Easy

SIZE:
5¾" x 13½".

MATERIALS:
One sheet of 7-count plastic canvas; 11 assorted-color ⅜-⅞" buttons; 1 yd. natural raffia; Two thin 5-6" twigs; Craft glue or glue gun; #3 pearl cotton or six-strand embroidery floss (for amounts see Color Key); Worsted-weight or plastic canvas yarn (for amounts see Color Key).

COLOR KEY: Slim Snowman

	#3 pearl cotton or floss			AMOUNT
■	Red			1 yd.
□	White			1 yd.

	Worsted-weight	Nylon Plus™	Need-loft®	YARN AMOUNT
■	Beige	#43	#40	25 yds.
■	Forest	#32	#29	25 yds.
□	White	#01	#41	20 yds.
□	Dk. Red	#20	#01	6 yds.
■	Black	#02	#00	3 yds.
■	Dusty Blue	#38	#34	3 yds.

STITCH KEY:
— Backstitch/Straight Stitch

CUTTING INSTRUCTIONS:
A: For snowman, cut one according to graph.
B: For background, cut one 37 x 89 holes (no graph).

STITCHING INSTRUCTIONS:
1: Using colors and stitches indicated, work pieces according to graph and stitch pattern guide; fill in uncoded areas of A using white and Continental Stitch. With dk. red for B and with matching colors, Overcast edges.

2: Using red pearl cotton or six strands floss and embroidery stitches indicated, embroider mouth detail on A as indicated on graph.

3: Using smaller buttons for eyes and nose and larger buttons for body, with white pearl cotton or six strands floss, sew buttons to snowman (see photo).

NOTE: Cut raffia in half.

4: For hanger, knot one end of each strand of raffia; thread unknotted end of each strand from front to back through top of B according to Hanger Assembly Diagram. Tie unknotted ends together into a bow. Glue twigs to back of snowman and snowman to background as shown. ⊙

**Background
Stitch Pattern Guide**

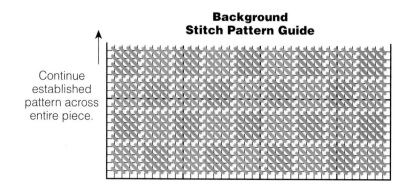

Continue established pattern across entire piece.

A – Snowman
(cut 1)
28 x 85 holes

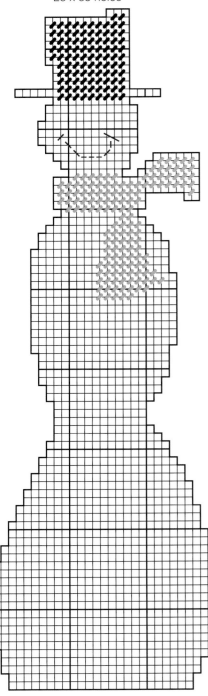

Hanger Assembly Diagram

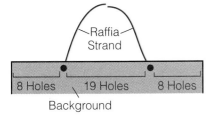

Raffia
Strand

| 8 Holes | 19 Holes | 8 Holes |

Background

Brighten up a room with this whimsical accent and fill acorn with goodies for all to enjoy.

Autumn Cache

Designed by Robin Petrina

LEVEL OF DIFFICULTY: Challenging

SIZE:
Base is 7½" x 10¾"; squirrel is 8½" tall.

MATERIALS:
Five sheets of 7-count plastic canvas; Two brown 12-mm animal eyes with washers; Polyester fiberfill; Craft glue or glue gun; Worsted-weight or plastic canvas yarn (for amounts see Color Key).

CUTTING INSTRUCTIONS:
NOTE: Graphs on pages 12-14 & 16.
A: For squirrel sides, cut two according to graph.
B: For squirrel chest, cut one according to graph.
C: For squirrel head and back, cut one according to graph.
D: For squirrel tail top, cut one according to graph.
E: For squirrel tail underside, cut one according to graph.
F: For squirrel arm pieces, cut four according to graph.
G: For squirrel leg pieces, cut four according to graph.
H: For squirrel ears, cut two according to graph.
I: For acorn lid side, cut one according to graph.
J: For acorn lid handle top, cut one 1 x 1 hole (no graph).
K: For acorn shell side, cut one according to graph.
L: For acorn shell bottom, cut one according to graph.
M: For leaves, cut eighteen according to graph.
N: For base top and backing, cut two (one for top and one for backing) according to graph.

STITCHING INSTRUCTIONS:
NOTE: Backing N piece is not worked.
1: Using colors and stitches indicated, work A (one on opposite side of canvas), B-E, F and G (two each on opposite side of canvas), H, I and K (overlap ends as indicated on graphs and work through both thicknesses at overlap areas to join), L, M and top N pieces according to graphs. Using black and embroidery stitches indicated, embroider nose detail on C as indicated on graph.

2: For arms and legs, holding two of each F and G pieces wrong sides together, with silver, Whipstitch together. For each ear, holding edges of one H wrong sides together, Whipstitch X edges together. (Right side of stitching will be on outside of ear.); Overcast unfinished edges. Insert one eye into cutout on each A piece and secure with washer. For squirrel body, with matching colors, Whipstitch A-E pieces together according to Squirrel Assembly Diagram, stuffing with fiberfill before closing.

3: For leaves, with dk. orange, Overcast edges of four M pieces; work stitches according to graph. Substituting colors, work remaining M pieces as above as follows: four in dk. rust and five each in dk. red and tangerine. For base, holding backing N to wrong side of base top, with forest, Whipstitch together.

4: For acorn, with dk. brown for shell and sand for lid, Whipstitch X and Y edges of K and I together as indicated. For shell, Whipstitch L to K at gathered X edges. For lid, Whipstitch J to I at gathered Y edges. Overcast unfinished edges of lid and shell.

5: For squirrel, glue arms, legs and ears to squirrel body and one dk. red leaf to inside of squirrel's left arm as shown in photo. Glue squirrel, acorn shell and remaining leaves to base as shown; place lid on shell. ⊕

Autumn Cache
Instructions & photo on pages 10 & 11

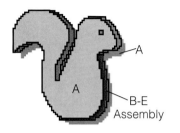

Squirrel Assembly Diagram

Step 1:
Whipstitch B-E
pieces together.

A

A

B-E
Assembly

Step 2: Holding
A pieces wrong
sides together
with B-E
assembly
between,
Whipstitch
together.

COLOR KEY: Autumn Cache

	Worsted-weight	Nylon Plus™	Need-loft®	YARN AMOUNT
	Silver	#40	#37	2½ oz.
	Forest	#32	#29	39 yds.
	Dk. Brown	#36	#15	28 yds.
	Sand	#47	#16	19 yds.
	Black	#02	#00	1 yd.
	Dk. Orange	#18	#52	1 yd.
	Dk. Red	#20	#01	1 yd.
	Dk. Rust	#16	#10	1 yd.
	Tangerine	#15	#11	1 yd.

STITCH KEY:

— Backstitch/Straight Stitch

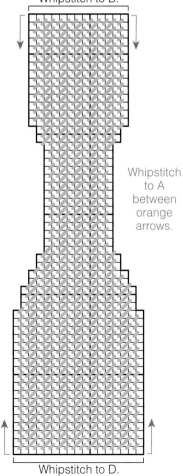

**E – Squirrel
Tail Underside**
(cut 1)
17 x 55 holes
Whipstitch to B.

Whipstitch
to A
between
orange
arrows.

Whipstitch to D.

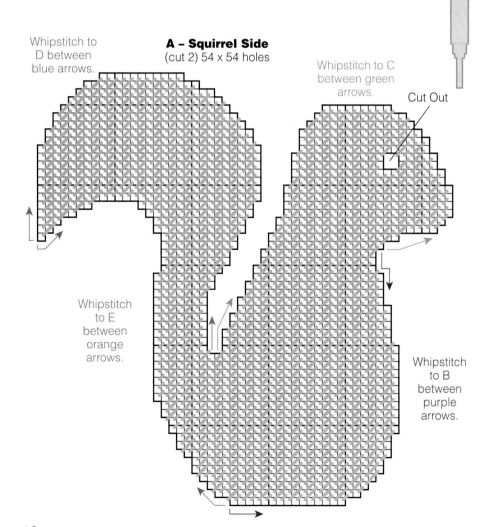

Whipstitch to
D between
blue arrows.

A – Squirrel Side
(cut 2) 54 x 54 holes

Whipstitch to C
between green
arrows.

Cut Out

Whipstitch
to E
between
orange
arrows.

Whipstitch
to B
between
purple
arrows.

H – Squirrel Ear
(cut 2) 5 x 5 holes

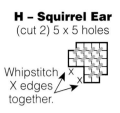

Whipstitch
X edges
together.

G – Squirrel Leg Piece
(cut 4)
18 x 19 holes

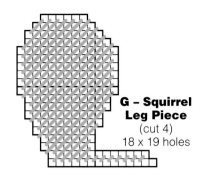

F – Squirrel Arm Piece
(cut 4)
9 x 17 holes

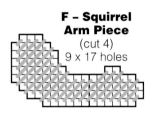

C – Squirrel Head & Back
(cut 1)
11 x 72 holes

Whipstitch to D.

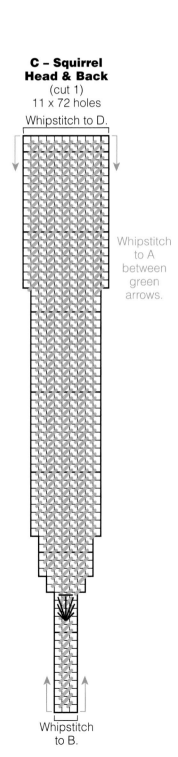

Whipstitch to A between green arrows.

Whipstitch to B.

D – Squirrel Tail Top
(cut 1) 17 x 75 holes

Whipstitch to E.

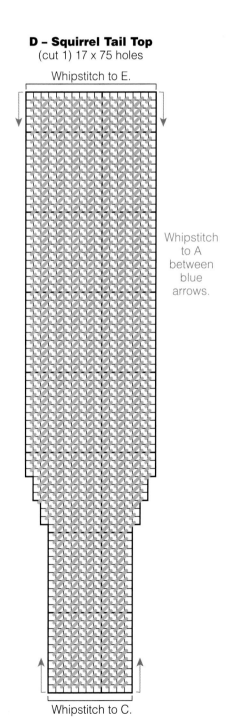

Whipstitch to A between blue arrows.

Whipstitch to C.

B – Squirrel Chest
(cut 1)
13 x 49 holes

Whipstitch to C.

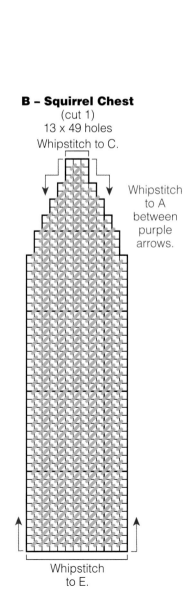

Whipstitch to A between purple arrows.

Whipstitch to E.

Autumn Cache
Instructions & photo on pages 10 & 11

I – Acorn Lid Side
(cut 1) 24 x 90 holes

Lap Under

X

Y

Y

Whipstitch
X edges,
then Y
edges
together.

X

X

Y

Y

X

X

X

X

Y

Y

X

X

X

X

Lap Over

K – Acorn Shell Side (cut 1) 29 x 84 holes

Lap Over

X

X

Whipstitch
X edges
together.

X

X

X

X

X

X

X

X

X

X

X

X

Lap Under

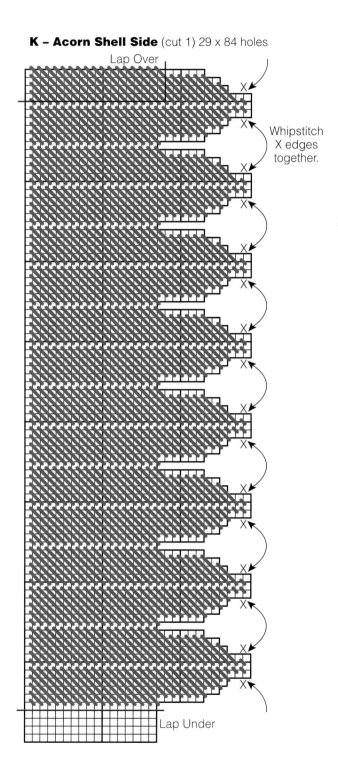

14

COUNTRY JAMBOREE

Heart & Home

Designed by Debi Yorston

LEVEL OF DIFFICULTY: Easy

SIZE:
Each is 5" square, not including hanger.

MATERIALS:
½ sheet 7-count plastic canvas; one dk. blue and one peach ½" button; one dk. pink and two lt. blue ⅝" buttons; two pink ¾" buttons; two ½-yd. lengths of black wire; Pencil; Sewing needle; #3 pearl cotton or six-strand embroidery floss (for amount see Color Key on page 16); Worsted-weight or plastic canvas yarn (for amounts see Color Key).

CUTTING INSTRUCTIONS:
A: For heart and home motifs, cut one each according to graphs on page 16.

STITCHING INSTRUCTIONS:
1: Using colors and stitches indicated, work pieces according to graphs; with eggshell, Overcast edges.

2: Using pearl cotton or six strands floss and Straight Stitch, embroider detail on heart motif A as indicated on graph. With sewing needle and blue pearl cotton or floss, sew dk. blue, peach and dk. pink buttons to heart as shown in photo.

3: For each hanger, wrap center of one wire around pencil 2-3 times to curl; remove pencil. Using pink buttons for heart and lt. blue buttons for home motif, insert one end of one wire from back to front through each cutout on one A and through one hole in one button. Curl wire ends to secure as shown.

15

Heart & Home

Instructions & photo on page 15

<table>
COLOR KEY: Heart & Home						
#3 pearl cotton or floss		**AMOUNT**		Royal	#09 #32	4 yds.
Blue		2 yds.		Dk. Royal #07 #48		2 yds.
				Gray #23 #38		2 yds.
Worsted-weight	Nylon Plus™	Need-loft®	YARN AMOUNT	Black #02 #00		1/4 yd.
Eggshell	#24	#39	40 yds.	**STITCH KEY:**		
Pink	#11	#07	6 yds.	— Backstitch/Straight Stitch		
</table>

A – Heart Motif
(cut 1) 33 x 33 holes

Cut out gray areas.

A – Home Motif
(cut 1) 33 x 33 holes

Cut out gray areas.

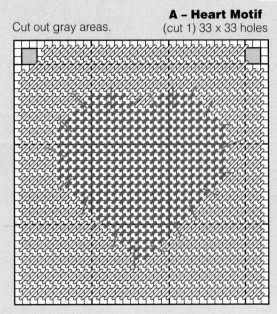

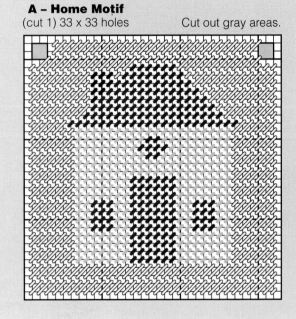

Autumn Cache

Instructions & photo on pages 10 & 11

N – Base Top & Backing (cut 2) 49 x 70 holes

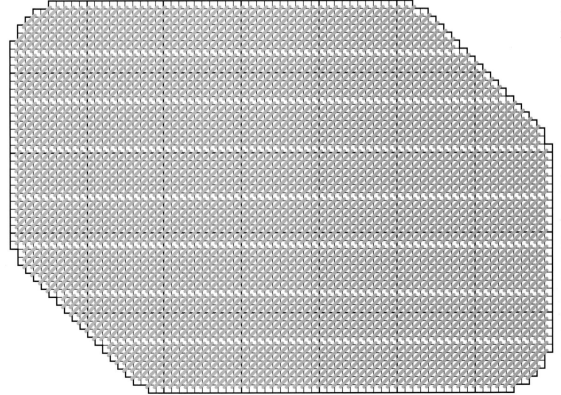

L – Acorn Shell Bottom
(cut 1)
9 x 9 holes

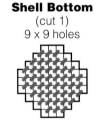

M – Leaf
(cut 18)
7 x 8 holes

16

Log Cabin Set

Designed by Nancy Marshall

Instructions on next page

Log Cabin Set

Photo on page 17

LEVEL OF DIFFICULTY: Challenging

SIZE:

Place Mat is 11" x 18¼"; Trivet is 7⅛" square; Napkin Ring is 2" across; Small Holder is 3" across x 2⅞" tall; Medium Holder is 4¾" across x 2" tall; Large Holder is 5½" across x 1¼" tall.

MATERIALS:

Two sheets of 5-count plastic canvas; One 3", one 4½" and one 6" plastic canvas circle; 45"-wide cotton print fabric (for amounts see Color Key).

CUTTING INSTRUCTIONS:

A: For Place Mat, cut one 55 x 90 holes.
B: For Trivet, cut one 35 x 35 holes.
C: For Napkin Ring, cut one 7 x 32 holes.
D: For Small Holder side, cut one 13 x 46 holes (no graph).
E: For Small Holder base, use 3" circle (no graph).
F: For Medium Holder side, cut one 9 x 70 holes (no graph).
G: For Medium Holder base, use 4½" circle (no graph).
H: For Large Holder side, cut one 5 x 85 holes (no graph).
I: For Large Holder base, cut 6" circle according to Cutting Guide.

FABRIC PREPARATION INSTRUCTIONS:

NOTE: If desired, pre-wash fabric in cool water.
1: For fabric strips, measuring along one selvage edge of fabric, mark every ¾" and snip with sharp scissors to begin tear. (If selvage will not tear easily, trim off with scissors before snipping.)

2: Holding fabric firmly with both hands, starting at cut, tear into strips. Discard first and last strips if not correct width. Remove any long threads from strips.

STITCHING INSTRUCTIONS:

NOTES: To thread needle, fold one short end of strip in half and slide through eye of needle. Handle strips carefully to prevent excessive fraying.

E, G and I pieces are not worked.
1: Using colors and stitches indicated, work A-D, F and H according to graphs and stitch pattern guides. With matching colors, Whipstitch ends of C and each holder side together. With ecru, Overcast edges of A and B pieces.

2: With red for Small Holder, blue for Medium Holder and green for Large Holder, Whipstitch D to E, F to G and H to I. With contrasting colors, Overcast edges of holders. For napkin ring, with tan, Overcast edges of C. ⊙

I – Cutting Guide

Step 1:
Cut away outside row of holes.

Step 2:
Cut out every other bar of next row carefully.

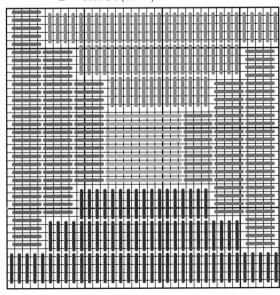

B – Trivet (cut 1) 35 x 35 holes

Small Holder
Stitch Pattern Guide

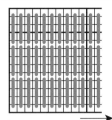

Continue established pattern across entire piece.

Medium Holder
Stitch Pattern Guide

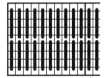

Continue established pattern across entire piece.

Large Holder
Stitch Pattern Guide

Continue established pattern across entire piece.

Napkin Ring
Stitch Pattern Guide

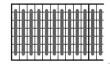

Continue established pattern across entire piece.

COLOR KEY: Log Cabin Set

45"-wide fabric	AMOUNT
⬜ Green Print	1$\frac{1}{4}$ yds.
⬛ Red Print	1 yd.
▨ Blue Print	$\frac{1}{3}$ yd.
▥ Ecru Print	$\frac{1}{3}$ yd.
▦ Tan Print	$\frac{1}{4}$ yd.

A – Place Mat (cut 1) 55 x 90 holes

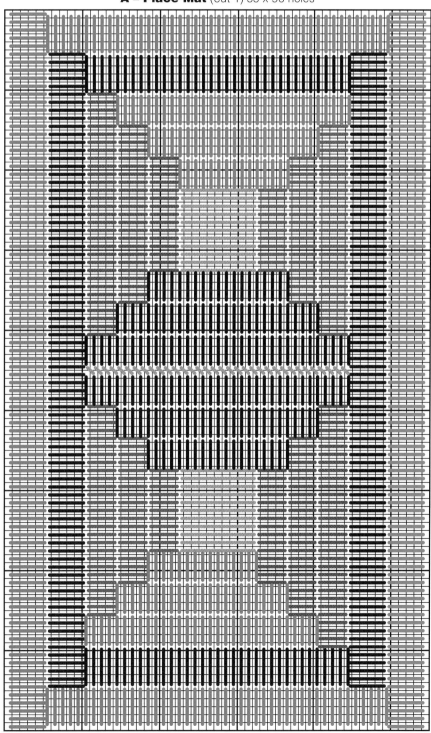

COUNTRY JAMBOREE

Homemade Love

Designed by Carol Nartowicz

LEVEL OF DIFFICULTY: Challenging

SIZE:
9¾" x 10¼".

MATERIALS:
Three sheets of 7-count plastic canvas; Two 3" metal cookie cutters; ¾ yd. white ¼" satin ribbon; Monofilament fishing line; Worsted-weight or plastic canvas yarn (for amounts see Color Key).

CUTTING INSTRUCTIONS:
NOTE: Graphs continued on page 23.
A: For front and backing, cut two (one for front and one for backing) according to graph.
B: For rolling pin pieces #1, cut two according to graph.
C: For rolling pin pieces #2, cut three according to graph.
D: For rolling pin pieces #3, cut two 6 x 36 holes (no graph).
E: For rolling pin pieces #4, cut three 4 x 36 holes (no graph).
F: For rolling pin pieces #5, cut two 2 x 36 holes (no graph).

STITCHING INSTRUCTIONS:

NOTE: Backing A and B-F pieces are not worked.

1: Using colors and stitches indicated, work front A (omit indicated rolling pin area) according to graph.

2: For rolling pin, assemble B-F pieces according to Rolling Pin Assembly Diagram on page 23; using colors and stitches indicated, work over all thicknesses according to B graph. Holding rolling pin assembly to front A as indicated, with matching colors, Whipstitch ends of roller and pin to A; using a double strand in colors indicated and Long Stitch, work over rolling pin assembly and through front A according to A graph.

3: Holding backing A to wrong side of front A, with sail blue, Whipstitch together.

NOTE: Cut ribbon in half.

4: To attach each cookie cutter, thread ends of one ribbon from back to front through one set of indicated holes; thread cookie cutter on ribbon and tie ends into a bow. ⊙

COLOR KEY: Homemade Love			
Worsted-weight	**Nylon Plus™**	**Need-loft®**	**YARN AMOUNT**
Sail Blue	#04	#35	40 yds.
Maple	#35	#13	12 yds.
Dk. Royal	#07	#48	8 yds.
Red	#19	#02	5 yds.
White	#01	#41	4 yds.

STITCH KEY:
- — Backstitch/Straight Stitch
- ☐ Unworked Area/Rolling Pin Attachment
- ✦ Ribbon Attachment

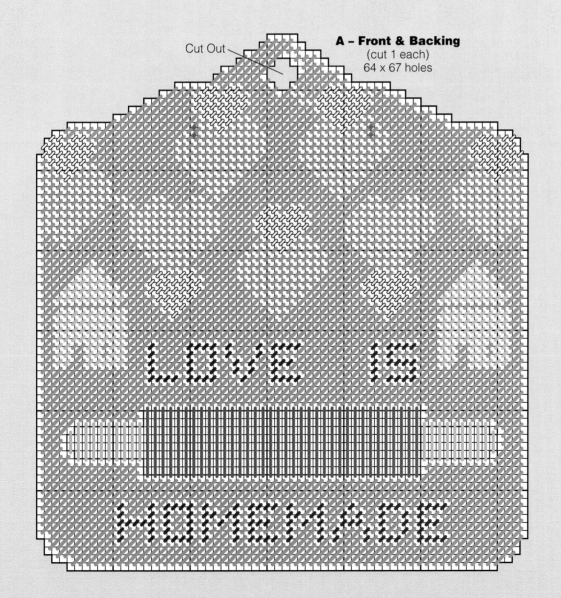

Cut Out

A – Front & Backing
(cut 1 each)
64 x 67 holes

Ginger Love

Designed by Michele Wilcox

LEVEL OF DIFFICULTY: Easy

SIZE:
Each figure is 4¾" x 7".

MATERIALS:
½ sheet of 7-count plastic canvas; Two decorative tan and two red ⅝" buttons; 12" grapevine wreath; 2 yds. 1½" Christmas plaid craft ribbon; Craft glue or glue gun; #3 pearl cotton or six-strand embroidery floss (for amounts see Color Key); Worsted-weight or plastic canvas yarn (for amounts see Color Key).

CUTTING INSTRUCTIONS:
A: For gingerbread man, cut one according to graph.
B: For gingerbread woman, cut one according to graph.

STITCHING INSTRUCTIONS:
1: Using colors indicated and Continental Stitch, work pieces according to graphs; fill in uncoded areas using camel and Continental Stitch. With matching colors, Overcast edges.

2: Using black pearl cotton or six strands floss and embroidery stitches indicated, embroider facial detail as indicated on graphs. With white pearl cotton or six strands floss, sew tan buttons to vest and red buttons to dress as shown in photo.

3: Wrap ribbon around wreath and tie ends in a bow as shown. Glue figures to wreath as shown. ⊙

STITCH KEY:
— Backstitch/Straight Stitch
● French Knot

COLOR KEY: Ginger Love

#3 pearl cotton or floss			AMOUNT
■ Black			2 yds.
□ White			1 yd.

Worsted-weight	Nylon Plus™	Need-loft®	YARN AMOUNT
□ Camel	#34	#43	20 yds.
□ White	#01	#41	8 yds.
□ Dk. Green	#31	#27	5 yds.
■ Dk. Red	#20	#01	2 yds.

A – Gingerbread Man
(cut 1)
31 x 46 holes

B – Gingerbread Woman
(cut 1)
31 x 46 holes

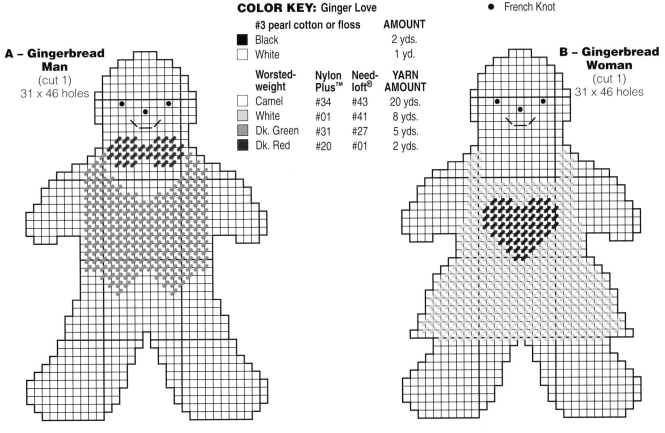

Homemade Love
Instructions & photo on page 20

B – Rolling Pin Piece #1 (cut 2) 8 x 56 holes

Rolling Pin Assembly Diagram
(Pieces are shown in different colors for contrast)

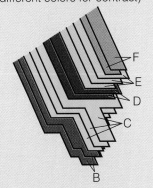

COLOR KEY: Homemade Love

Worsted-weight	Nylon Plus™	Need-loft®	YARN AMOUNT
Sail Blue	#04	#35	40 yds.
Maple	#35	#13	12 yds.
Dk. Royal	#07	#48	8 yds.
Red	#19	#02	5 yds.
White	#01	#41	4 yds.

STITCH KEY:
— Backstitch/Straight Stitch
☐ Unworked Area/Rolling Pin Attachment
✦ Ribbon Attachment

C – Rolling Pin Piece #2 (cut 3) 8 x 54 holes

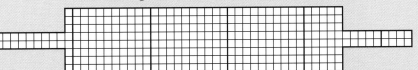

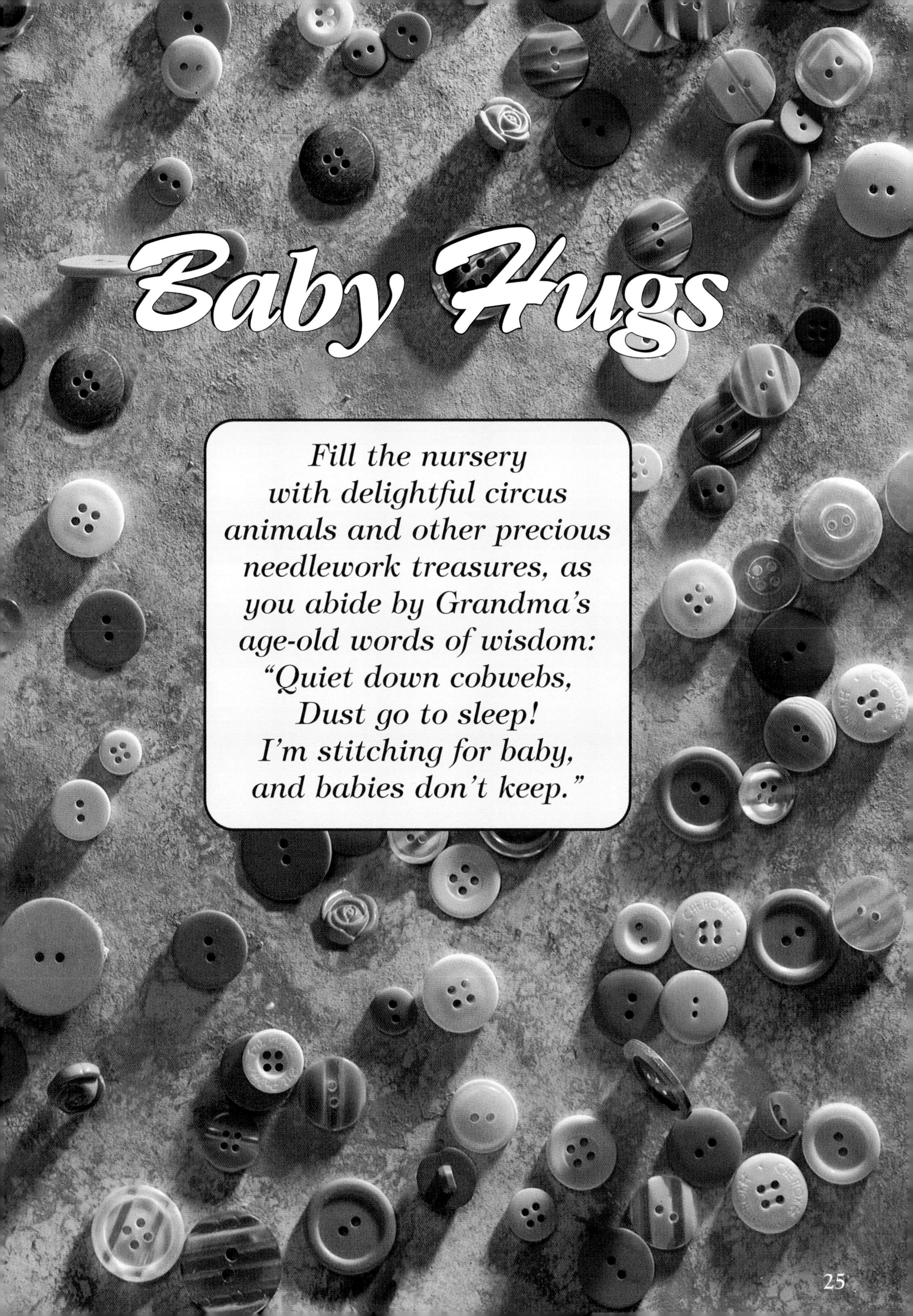

Baby Hugs

Fill the nursery
with delightful circus
animals and other precious
needlework treasures, as
you abide by Grandma's
age-old words of wisdom:
"Quiet down cobwebs,
Dust go to sleep!
I'm stitching for baby,
and babies don't keep."

Baby Shower

Designed by Diane T. Ray

LEVEL OF DIFFICULTY: Average

SIZE:
10¾" x 13⅝", not including message.

MATERIALS:
2¼ sheets of neon blue 7-count plastic canvas; ¼ sheet each of neon yellow, neon pink and white 7-count plastic canvas; Scrap of clear 10-count plastic canvas; One 3" x 4¾" piece of clear plastic and one computer-generated or handmade sign; Craft glue or glue gun; Worsted-weight or plastic canvas yarn (for amounts see Color Key on page 29).

CUTTING INSTRUCTIONS:
NOTES: Graphs on pages 28 & 29. Use 10-count for F pieces and 7-count canvas for remaining pieces.

A: For front and back, cut two (one for front and one for back) from blue according to graph.

B: For ear, cut one from pink according to graph.

C: For front and back toenails, cut one each from pink according to graphs.

D: For tail, cut one from pink according to graph.

E: For rug, cut one from yellow according to graph.

F: For tassels, cut seven according to graph.

G: For letter block backs, from white cut seven for boy announcement or eight for girl announcement 11 x 11 holes (no graph).

H: For letter block borders, from desired color(s) cut seven for boy announcement or eight for girl announcement according to graph.

I: For letters, cut number needed from black according to graphs.

J: For long links, cut two from black according to graph.

K: For short links, from black cut six for boy announcement or seven for girl announcement according to graph.

STITCHING INSTRUCTIONS:
NOTE: One A for back, B, D and G-I pieces are not worked.

1: Using colors and stitches indicated, work one A for front according to graph. Positioning C pieces on front A as indicated on graph, using black and Continental Stitch, work through both thicknesses as one according to C graphs; Whipstitch top and bottom edges of toenails to front A. Positioning E on front A as indicated, using colors and stitches indicated, work through both thicknesses as one according to E graph; do not Overcast edges.

NOTE: Separate remaining bt. purple into 2-ply or nylon plastic canvas yarn into 1-ply strands.

2: Using bt. purple and stitches indicated, work F pieces according to graphs; Overcast edges, tacking F pieces to E and front A through both thicknesses at ▲ holes as indicated to secure.

3: Positioning B on front A as indicated, with black, Whipstitch together through both thicknesses.

4: Holding back A to wrong side of worked piece, with yellow for top edges of rug as shown in photo and with black, Whipstitch together as indicated, positioning and Whipstitching D to right side of A as you work as indicated.

5: Insert plastic and sign through small cutouts on back of A pieces so they rest between rug and A pieces (see photo).

6: For message, assemble G-K pieces according to Blocks Assembly Diagram.

7: Hang as desired. ☺

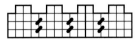

Baby Shower

Instructions & photo on pages 26 & 27

B – Ear
(cut 1 from pink) 13 x 31 holes

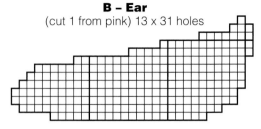

C – Front Toenails
(cut 1 from pink) 4 x 16 holes

C – Back Toenails
(cut 1 from pink) 4 x 20 holes

A – Front & Back
(cut 1 each) 70 x 89 holes

Whipstitch between arrows.

Cut Out

Whipstitch between arrows.

Cut Out

D – Tail
(cut 1 from pink)
5 x 12 holes

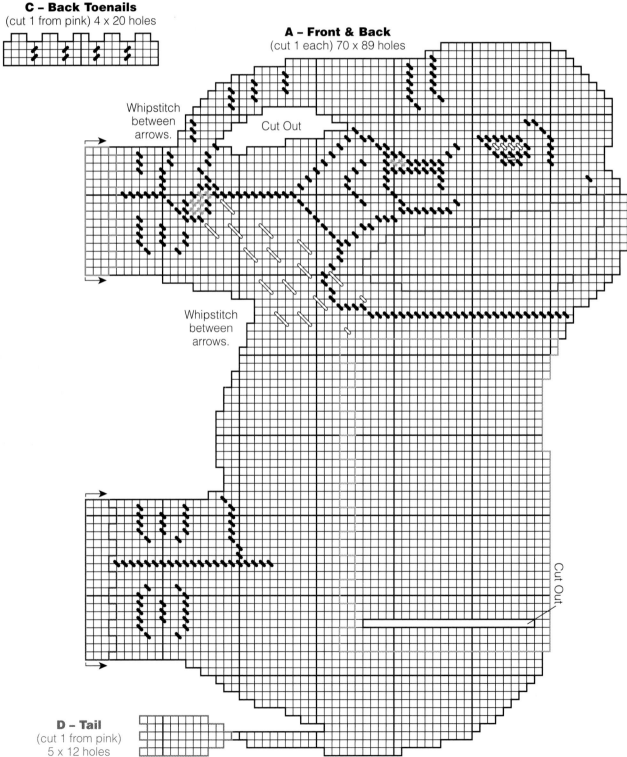

K – Short Link
(from black cut 6
for boy or 7 for girl)
2 x 2 holes

Cut bar here.

J – Long Link
(cut 2 from black)
2 x 5 holes

Cut bar here.

E – Rug
(cut 1 from yellow) 28 x 39 holes

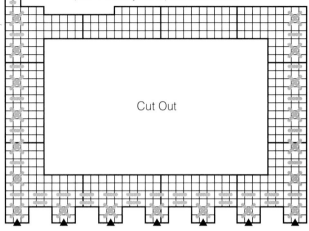

Cut Out

H – Letter Block Border
(cut 7 for boy or 8 for girl)
11 x 11 holes

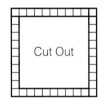

Cut Out

I – Letters
(cut number needed from black) 5 x 7 holes

Cut out lt. blue areas carefully.

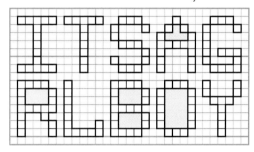

F – Tassel
(cut 7 from
10-count)
5 x 10 holes

COLOR KEY: Baby Shower

Worsted-weight	Nylon Plus™	Need-loft®	YARN AMOUNT
■ Black	#02	#00	11 yds.
▦ Bt. Purple	–	#64	4 yds.
▦ Bt. Pink	–	#62	1 yd.
☐ Bt. Yellow	–	#63	1 yd.
▨ White	#01	#41	1 yd.

STITCH KEY:

☐ Front Toenails Attachment
☐ Back Toenails Attachment
▲ Tassel Attachment
☐ Rug Attachment
☐ Ear Attachment

Blocks Assembly Diagram
(Some pieces are shown in different colors for contrast.)

Step 1:
For each block, omitting outer corners of block backs and borders, glue one of each G-I pieces together.

(magnified view)

Step 2:
Using K pieces between letters and at ends of message and J pieces between words, link blocks together by inserting one J or K piece from front to back through both thicknesses at upper corners of each block.

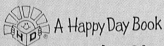

Alphabet Frames

Designed by Susie Spier Maxfield

LEVEL OF DIFFICULTY: Average

SIZE:

Each Bookend is 2" x 5⅛" x 6" tall and covers a standard-size metal bookend; Girl Bookend has a 2" x 2¾" photo window; Boy Bookend has one 1" x 1¼" and one 1¾" x 2¾" photo window; Each balloon is 1½" x 1¾" and has a ⅝" x ⅝" photo window.

MATERIALS FOR ONE:

Two sheets of 7-count plastic canvas; Scraps of white felt; ⅔ yd. of white ½" eyelet lace (for Girl Bookend); One small flocked bear and three miniature gift boxes (for Boy Bookend) or one small baby doll and three wooden alphabet blocks (for Girl Bookend); Craft glue or glue gun; Worsted-weight or plastic canvas yarn (for amounts see individual Color Keys on page 32 & 33).

GIRL BOOKEND

CUTTING INSTRUCTIONS:

NOTE: Graphs on page 33.
A: For cover front, cut one according to graph.
B: For cover backing and lining, cut two (one for backing and one for lining) 33 x 38 holes (no graph).
C: For cover bottom, cut one 11 x 33 holes.
D: For heart balloon frames, cut three according to graph.
E: For alphabet hearts, cut one each according to graphs.
F: For balloon frame backings, using one D as a pattern, cut three from felt ⅛" smaller at all edges.

STITCHING INSTRUCTIONS:

NOTE: B pieces are not worked.
1: Using colors and stitches indicated, work A and C pieces according to graphs. Using red, green and lemon and Continental Stitch, work one D in each color; using lavender and Continental Stitch, work E pieces. With pink, Overcast cutout edges of A; with matching

colors and leaving a 4" length of yarn at center bottom of each balloon (see photo) for string, Overcast edges of D and E pieces.

NOTE: Separate remaining red into 2-ply or nylon plastic canvas into 1-ply strands.

2: Using 2-ply (or 1-ply) red and Backstitch, embroider letters on E pieces as indicated on graphs.

3: For cover, with pink, Whipstitch A-C pieces together according to Frame Assembly Diagram on page 33.

NOTE: Cut lace into three 8" lengths.

4: Slide metal bookend inside cover between cover backing and lining. Glue one piece of lace to wrong side around outer edge of each alphabet heart (see photo); glue wood blocks together, then glue block assembly and baby doll to cover bottom and alphabet hearts to cover front as shown.

5: For each balloon frame backing, omitting top edges so photo can slide into frame, glue sides and bottom of one F to wrong side of each E. Tie ends of strings together into a knot and trim ends (see photo); glue balloons to cover as shown.

BOY BOOKEND

CUTTING INSTRUCTIONS:

NOTES: Graphs on page 32.
A: For cover front, cut one according to graph.
B-C: Follow Steps B and C of Girl Bookend.
D: For round balloon frames, cut three according to graph.
E: For alphabet letters, cut one each according to graphs.
F: Follow Step F of Girl Bookend.

STITCHING INSTRUCTIONS:

NOTE: B pieces are not worked.
1: Using colors and stitches indicated, work A and C pieces according to graphs. Using red, lt. yellow and lavender and Continental Stitch, work one of each D and E in each

Continued on next page

Alphabet Frames

Continued from page 31

Stitch, work one of each D and E in each color. With lt. green, Overcast cutout edges of A; with matching colors and leaving a 4" length of yarn at center bottom of each balloon (see photo) for string, Overcast edges of D and E pieces.

2: For cover, with lt. green, follow Step 3 of Girl Bookend on page 31.

3: Slide metal bookend inside cover between cover backing and lining. Glue bear and gift boxes to cover bottom and alphabet letters to cover front as shown.

4: Follow Step 5 of Girl Bookend.

A – Boy Bookend Cover Front
(cut 1) 33 x 38 holes

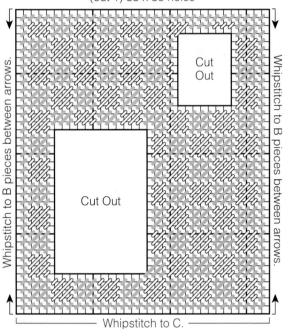

Whipstitch to B pieces between arrows.

Whipstitch to B pieces between arrows.

Cut Out

Cut Out

Whipstitch to C.

C – Boy Bookend Cover Bottom
(cut 1) 11 x 33 holes

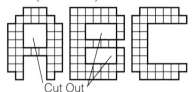

Whipstitch to A and backing B.

E – Boy Bookend Alphabet Letters
(cut 1 each) 7 x 9 holes

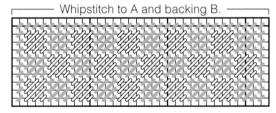

Cut Out

D – Boy Bookend
Round Balloon Frame
(cut 3) 9 x 11 holes

Cut Out

COLOR KEY: Boy Bookend

	Worsted-weight	Nylon Plus™	Need-loft®	YARN AMOUNT
▪	Lt. Green	#28	#26	20 yds.
▨	White	#01	#41	10 yds.
☐	Lavender	#22	#45	3 yds.
☐	Lt. Yellow	#42	#21	3 yds.
☐	Red	#19	#02	3 yds.

A – Girl Bookend Cover Front
(cut 1) 33 x 38 holes

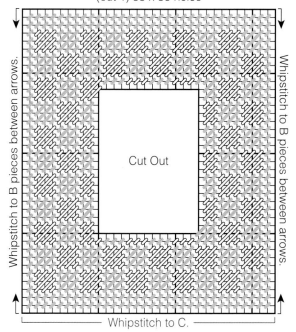

Whipstitch to B pieces between arrows.

Cut Out

Whipstitch to B pieces between arrows.

Whipstitch to C.

C – Girl Bookend Cover Bottom
(cut 1) 11 x 33 holes

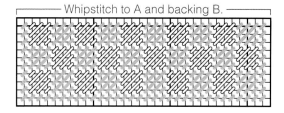

Whipstitch to A and backing B.

E – Girl Bookend Alphabet Hearts
(cut 1 each) 7 x 8 holes

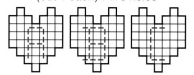

COLOR KEY: Girl Bookend

	Worsted-weight	Nylon Plus™	Need-loft®	YARN AMOUNT
	Pink	#11	#07	20 yds.
	White	#01	#41	10 yds.
	Lavender	#22	#45	6 yds.
	Red	#19	#02	2¹/₂ yds.
	Green	#58	#28	2 yds.
	Lemon	#25	#20	2 yds.

STITCH KEY:

— Backstitch/Straight Stitch

D – Girl Bookend Heart Balloon Frame
(cut 3) 9 x 11 holes

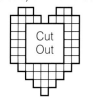

Cut Out

Frame Assembly Diagram
(Pieces are shown in different colors for contrast.)

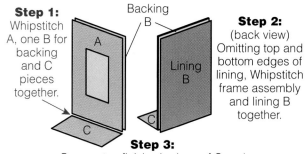

Step 1:
Whipstitch A, one B for backing and C pieces together.

Backing B

Step 2:
(back view) Omitting top and bottom edges of lining, Whipstitch frame assembly and lining B together.

A

Lining B

C

C

Step 3:
Overcast unfinished edges of C and unfinished top edges of lining B.

33

Animal Circus

Designed by Michele Wilcox

LEVEL OF DIFFICULTY: Easy

SIZE:
Each is 7⅝" x 9⅛", not
including hanger.

MATERIALS:
Two sheets of 7-count plastic canvas; 2
yds. dk. green ⅛" satin ribbon; Two ⅞"
flat buttons; #3 pearl cotton or six strand
embroidery floss (for amount see Color
Key); Worsted-weight or plastic canvas
yarn (for amounts see Color Key).

CUTTING INSTRUCTIONS:
NOTE: Elephant graph on page 36.
A: For Elephant and Giraffe motifs, cut two
(one for Elephant and one for Giraffe) 50 x
60 holes.

STITCHING INSTRUCTIONS:
1: Using colors indicated and Continental
Stitch, work pieces according to graphs; fill in
uncoded areas using white and Continental
Stitch. With pumpkin for Elephant and royal
for Giraffe, Overcast edges.

2: Using #3 pearl cotton or six strands floss,
Backstitch, Straight Stitch and French Knot,
embroider eyes, mouth, tail and ear outlines
as indicated on graphs.

3: Holding buttons to Elephant motif as indicated, with white, work one Cross Stitch
through button holes (see photo) and
through motif; secure ends.

NOTE: Cut ribbon into four ½-yd. lengths.

4: For each motif, thread one ½-yd. ribbon
through each ♦ hole at top of one motif as
indicated; pull ends to even. Tie all ribbon
ends together into a bow as desired or as
shown in photo to form hanger; if desired,
trim ends. ☺

COLOR KEY: Animal Circus

Embroidery floss			AMOUNT
Black			2 yds.

Worsted-weight	Nylon Plus™	Need-loft®	YARN AMOUNT
White	#01	#41	65 yds.
Sea Green	#37	#53	16 yds.
Pumpkin	#50	#12	14 yds.
Royal	#09	#32	12 yds.
Silver	#40	#37	12 yds.
Dk. Red	#20	#01	10 yds.
Yellow	#26	#57	8 yds.
Gold	#27	#17	4 yds.
Flesh	#14	#56	1 yd.

STITCH KEY:
- Backstitch/Straight Stitch
- French Knot
- Button Attachment

A – Giraffe Motif
(cut 1) 50 x 60 holes

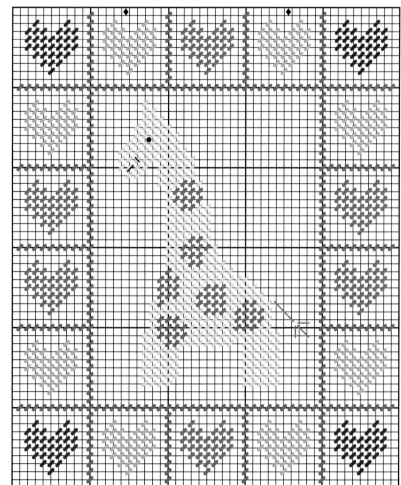

Animal Circus

Instructions on page 35

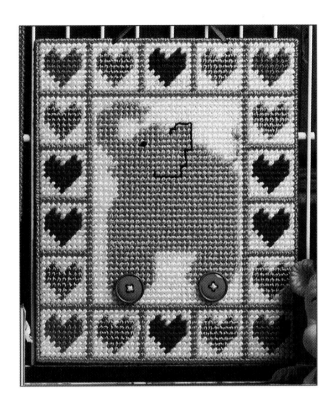

COLOR KEY: Animal Circus

	Embroidery floss			AMOUNT
■	Black			2 yds.

	Worsted-weight	Nylon Plus™	Need-loft®	YARN AMOUNT
☐	White	#01	#41	65 yds.
	Sea Green	#37	#53	16 yds.
	Pumpkin	#50	#12	14 yds.
	Royal	#09	#32	12 yds.
	Silver	#40	#37	12 yds.
	Dk. Red	#20	#01	10 yds.
	Yellow	#26	#57	8 yds.
	Gold	#27	#17	4 yds.
	Flesh	#14	#56	1 yd.

STITCH KEY:

— Backstitch/Straight Stitch
● French Knot
○ Button Attachment

A – Elephant Motif
(cut 1) 50 x 60 holes

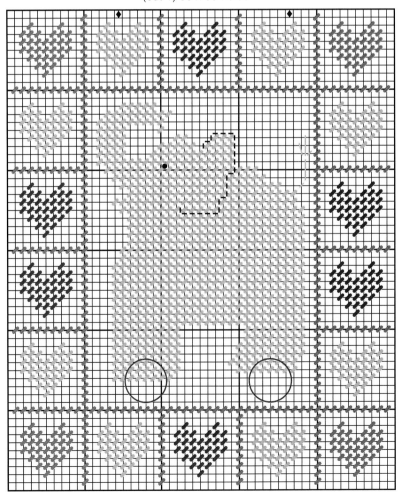

BABY HUGS

Musical Shelf Sitters

Designed by Sandra Miller Maxfield
& Susie Spier Maxfield

LEVEL OF DIFFICULTY: Average

SIZE:
Each is about 3¼" x 5¾" x 6" tall.

MATERIALS FOR ONE:
¾ sheet of 7-count plastic canvas; One blue, one green and one red 5-mm pom-pom (for Clown); One music button with tune of choice; Two music button spacers; One 2" x 6" and one 2" x 9" piece of cardboard; Craft glue or glue gun; Worsted-weight or plastic canvas yarn (for amounts see individual Color Keys on pages 39 & 40).

BEAR

CUTTING INSTRUCTIONS:
NOTE: Graphs on page 39.
A: For head, cut one according to graph.
B: For body front and back, cut one 12 x 15 for front and one according to graph for back (no front graph).
C: For body sides, cut two 4 x 15 holes (no graph).
D: For body top and bottom, cut two (one for top and one for bottom) 4 x 12 holes (no graph).
E: For ears, cut two according to graph.
F: For muzzle, cut one according to graph.
G: For bib, cut one according to graph.

STITCHING INSTRUCTIONS:
1: Using colors and stitches indicated, work A and E-G pieces according to graphs; fill in

Continued on page 38

uncoded areas of A and work B-D pieces using camel and Continental Stitch. With camel, Overcast cutout edges of back B and edges of E pieces. With tan, Overcast edges of F. With white, Overcast edges of G as indicated on graph; leaving a 9" tail at each top corner (see photo) for tie, with yellow, Overcast remaining edges of G.

2: Using black and embroidery stitches indicated, embroider eyes on A and nose and mouth on F as indicated.

3: For head, holding edges wrong sides together, with camel, Whipstitch Y edges and ends of A together as indicated; Whipstitch top and bottom openings closed. For body, Whipstitch and assemble B-D pieces, music button and spacers according to Body Assembly Diagram on page 40.

NOTE: Cut two 5-yd., two 7½-yd. and eight 6" lengths of camel.

4: For each arm, wrap one 5-yd. strand around length of 2" x 6" cardboard; slide loops off cardboard. Knot one 6" strand around center of loops; fold loops in half and tie one 6" strand around loops about 1½" from fold. Cut through loops at end near second tie; trim and fluff ends to form a pom-pom (see photo). Repeat for each leg, using larger cardboard and substituting one 7½-yd. for one 5-yd. strand.

5: Glue head, arms and legs to body and ears and muzzle to head (see photo). Glue bib to front and tie bib ties into a bow at back of body; if desired, glue ties to secure.

DOLL

CUTTING INSTRUCTIONS:
NOTE: Graphs on page 40.
A: For head, cut one according to graph.
B-D: Follow Steps B-D of Bear on page 37.
E: For dress, cut one according to graph.
F: For shoes, cut two according to graph.
G: For hands, cut two 2 x 3 holes (no graph).

STITCHING INSTRUCTIONS:
1: Using colors and stitches indicated, work A, E (overlap holes at ends as indicated on graph and work through both thicknesses at overlap areas to join) and F pieces according to graphs; fill in uncoded areas of A and work G pieces using pink and Continental Stitch. Using red and Continental Stitch, work B-D pieces. With white, Overcast edges of E as indicated; with matching colors, Overcast remaining edges of E, cutout edges of back B and edges of F and G pieces.

2: Using colors and embroidery stitches indicated, embroider eyes and mouth on A as indicated.

3: Substituting pink for camel on head and red for camel on body, follow Step 3 of Bear.

NOTE: Cut one 2½-yd. and one 3¾-yd. length each of red and white and eight 6" lengths of red.

4: For each arm, holding one of each color 2½-yd. strand together, wrap around length of 2" x 6" cardboard; slide loops off cardboard. Knot one 6" strand around center of loops; fold loops in half and tie one 6" strand around loops about 1½" from fold. Cut through loops at end near second tie; trim and fluff ends to form a pom-pom (see photo). Repeat for each leg, using larger cardboard and substituting one of each color 3¾-yd. strand for 2½-yd. strands.

5: Glue fold of each leg to lower edge on front of body. Slide dress over body; bending bodice area of dress over top of body and to back, tuck bodice tails of dress under skirt at back and glue dress to body to secure. Glue arms and head to body and hands and feet to arms and legs as shown.

NOTE: Cut three 1-yd. and twenty-four 6" lengths of cinnamon.

7: Wrap one 1-yd. strand loosely around pencil; glue one edge of loops to secure (see Loop Diagram on page 40). Before glue cools, slide loops off pencil and carefully place glued edge in a circle around doll's head, forming hair (see photo). Repeat with remaining 1-yd. strands to cover head, trimming sections as needed to fit. For each ponytail, knot one 6" strand around center of ten 6" strands; fold strands in half and tie one 6" strand around all strands about ½" from fold. Trim and fluff ends to form a pom-pom. Glue ponytails to hair as shown.

CLOWN

CUTTING INSTRUCTIONS:
NOTE: Graphs on page 40.
A: For head, cut one according to graph.
B-D: Follow Steps B-D of Bear.
E: For shoes, cut four according to graph.
F: For hands, cut two 2 x 3 holes (no graph).

STITCHING INSTRUCTIONS:

1: Using colors and stitches indicated, work A and E pieces according to graphs; fill in uncoded areas of A and work F pieces using white and Continental Stitch. Using yellow and Continental Stitch, work B-D pieces. With white, Overcast edges of F pieces. With yellow, Overcast cutout edges of back B.

2: Using colors and embroidery stitches indicated, embroider facial detail on A as indicated on graph. For each shoe, holding two E pieces wrong sides together, with cinnamon, Whipstitch together.

3: Substituting white for camel on head and yellow for camel on body, follow Step 3 of Bear.

NOTE: Cut one 1¼-yd. and one 2-yd. length each of yellow, turquoise, bt. green and orange and eight 6" lengths of yellow.

4: For each arm, holding one of each color 1¼-yd. strand together, wrap around length of 2" x 6" cardboard; slide loops off cardboard. Knot one 6" strand around center of loops; fold loops in half and tie one 6" strand around loops about 1½" from fold. Cut through loops at end near second tie; trim and fluff ends to form a pom-pom (see photo). Repeat for each leg, using larger cardboard and substituting one of each color 3¾-yd. strand for 1¼-yd. strands.

5: Glue head, arms, legs and 5-mm pom-poms to body as shown. Glue hands to arms and shoes to legs (see photo).

NOTE: Cut two 1-yd. lengths of orange.

6: Substituting orange for cinnamon and omitting ponytail instructions, follow Step 7 of Doll.

G – Bear Bib
(cut 1)
9 x 10 holes

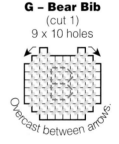

Overcast between arrows.

F – Bear Muzzle
(cut 1) 3 x 5 holes

E – Bear Ear
(cut 2)
3 x 4 holes

A – Bear Head
(cut 1) 12 x 24 holes
Whipstitch Y edges together.

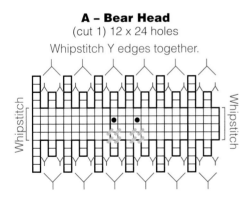

Whipstitch

Whipstitch

B – Bear Body Back
(cut 1) 12 x 15 holes

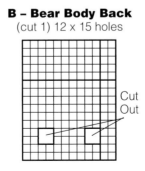

Cut
Out

COLOR KEY: Bear

Worsted-weight	Nylon Plus™	Need-loft®	YARN AMOUNT
Camel	#34	#43	46 yds.
Straw	#41	#19	3 yds.
Sand	#47	#16	1 yd.
White	#01	#41	1 yd.
Black	#02	#00	½ yd.
Pink	#11	#07	¼ yd.
Sail Blue	#04	#35	¼ yd.

STITCH KEY:

— Backstitch/Straight Stitch
• French Knot

Musical Shelf Sitters

Instructions & photo on page 37

COLOR KEY: Clown

	Worsted-weight	Nylon Plus™	Need-loft®	YARN AMOUNT
☐	Yellow	#26	#57	12 yds.
▨	Cinnamon	#44	#14	8 yds.
☐	Orange	#17	#58	6 yds.
☐	White	#01	#41	6 yds.
☐	Bt. Green	–	#61	4 yds.
☐	Turquoise	#03	#54	4 yds.
■	Black	#02	#00	1/4 yd.
▨	Pink	#11	#07	1/4 yd.
■	Red	#19	#02	1/4 yd.

STITCH KEY:

— Backstitch/Straight Stitch
● French Knot
× Cross Stitch

E – Clown Shoe
(cut 4)
5 x 9 holes

F – Doll Shoe
(cut 2)
5 x 9 holes

A – Clown Head
(cut 1) 12 x 24 holes

Whipstitch Y edges together.

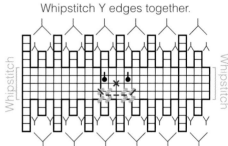

Whipstitch

Whipstitch

A – Doll Head
(cut 1) 12 x 24 holes

Whipstitch Y edges together.

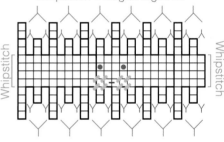

Whipstitch

Whipstitch

Body Assembly Diagram

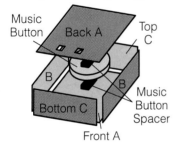

Music Button
Back A
Top C
B
B
Music Button Spacer
Bottom C
Front A

Loop Diagram

E – Doll Dress
(cut 1)
31 x 32 holes

Lap Under
Overcast between arrows.
Cut Out
Overcast between arrows.
Overcast between arrows.
Lap Over
Overcast between arrows.

COLOR KEY: Doll

	Worsted-weight	Nylon Plus™	Need-loft®	YARN AMOUNT
■	Red	#19	#02	34 yds.
☐	White	#01	#01	26 yds.
▨	Cinnamon	#44	#14	12 yds.
☐	Lt. Pink	#10	#08	10 yds.
▨	Turquoise	#03	#54	6 yds.
▨	Pink	#11	#07	1/4 yd.

STITCH KEY:

— Backstitch/Straight Stitch
● French Knot

Twilight Teddy

Designed by
Debbie Tabor

Instructions on next page

Twilight Teddy

Photo on page 41

LEVEL OF DIFFICULTY: Easy

SIZE:
3⅜" x 9¾" x 13" tall, not including handles.

MATERIALS:
Three sheets of 7-count plastic canvas; Metallic cord (for amount see Color Key); Six-strand embroidery floss (for amount see Color Key); Plastic glow lacing (for amounts see Color Key); Worsted-weight or plastic canvas yarn (for amounts see Color Key).

CUTTING INSTRUCTIONS:
A: For front and back, cut two (one for front and one for back) 64 x 85 holes (no back graph).
B: For sides, cut two 21 x 85 holes (no graph).

C: For bottom, cut one 21 x 64 holes (no graph).
D: For handles, cut two 5 x 60 holes (no graph).

STITCHING INSTRUCTIONS:
1: Using colors and stitches indicated and working lacing stitches first, work one A for front according to graph; fill in uncoded areas using multi-black cord and Continental Stitch. Using turquoise and stitches indicated, work remaining A for back, B and D pieces according to background border pattern established on A, and work C pieces according to Side Stitch Pattern Guide; Overcast long edges of D pieces.

2: Using six strands floss, Backstitch and Cross Stitch, embroider bear facial features and outlines as indicated on A graph.

3: With turquoise, Whipstitch A-C pieces together, forming Tote; Overcast unfinished edges, attaching short edges of D pieces to front and back as you work as indicated. ⊙

Side Stitch Pattern Guide

Continue established pattern up entire length of piece.

COLOR KEY: Twilight Teddy

	Metallic cord	AMOUNT
☐	Multi-Black	62 yds.

	Embroidery floss	AMOUNT
■	Black	6 yds.

	Plastic glow lacing	AMOUNT
▧	Yellow	52 yds.
▦	Aqua	2 yds.
▦	Blue	2 yds.
▦	Green	2 yds.
▦	Pink	2 yds.
■	Tangerine	2 yds.

	Worsted-weight	Nylon Plus™	Need-loft®	YARN AMOUNT
▦	Turquoise	#03	#54	4 oz.
▦	Camel	#34	#43	24 yds.

STITCH KEY:
— Backstitch/Straight Stitch
× Cross Stitch

A – Front
(cut 1) 64 x 85 holes

Handle Attachment

Springtime Fresh

An open window and gentle spring breezes fill the room with sounds of children's laughter from the passing Easter parade. Stitch a batch of loveable bunnies, then dress up in your finest spring attire, gather up your needlework basket and follow the sounds along the bunny trail.

April Showers

Designed by Sandra Miller Maxfield

LEVEL OF DIFFICULTY: Challenging

SIZE:
8" across x 8" tall, including handle.

MATERIALS:
Two sheets of 7-count plastic canvas; One 9½" plastic canvas radial circle; Craft glue or glue gun; Worsted-weight or plastic canvas yarn (for amounts see Color Key).

CUTTING INSTRUCTIONS:
A: For fronts and backs, cut eight each according to graphs.
B: For bottom, cut away outer six rows of holes from circle to measure 7⅝" across (no graph).

C: For handle, cut one 5 x 90 holes (no graph).

STITCHING INSTRUCTIONS:
NOTE: B piece is not worked.
1: Using colors indicated and Continental Stitch, work two A pieces according to each A graph. Substituting pink, purple and straw for royal, and lavender, lt. pink and lt. yellow for sail blue, work two of each remaining A in each color according to graphs. With silver for tips and with royal, Overcast top edges of blue A pieces only as indicated on graphs.

2: Using pink and Slanted Gobelin Stitch over narrow width, work C; Overcast unfinished edges of handle.

3: With silver for umbrella tips and with matching main colors, Whipstitch and assemble pieces as indicated and according to Basket Assembly Diagram. ⊡

Basket Assembly Diagram

NOTE: Position blue umbrellas on opposite sides.

Handle

NOTE: Tab is inserted in between front A and back A.

Step 1:
To join motifs, holding one of each A wrong sides together, insert tab between front and back of adjacent motif; working through all thicknesses as needed to join, Whipstitch fronts and backs together as indicated.

Step 2:
Whipstitch assembly and B together as indicated, Overcasting unfinished edges of bottom as you work.

Step 3:
Glue ends of handle inside openings on blue umbrellas to secure.

Back A

Front A

B

COLOR KEY: April Showers

	Worsted-weight	Nylon Plus™	Need-loft®	YARN AMOUNT
☐	Pink	#11	#07	20 yds.
▨	Silver	#40	#37	19 yds.
☐	Purple	#21	#46	14 yds.
■	Royal	#09	#32	14 yds.
☐	Straw	#41	#19	14 yds.
☐	Lavender	#22	#45	8 yds.
☐	Lt. Pink	#10	#08	8 yds.
☐	Lt. Yellow	#42	#21	8 yds.
☐	Sail Blue	#04	#35	8 yds.

STITCH KEY:

☐ Tab Between

A – Front
(cut 8) 19 x 23 holes
Overcast blue pieces.

Whipstitch to back tab.

Whipstitch to back tab.

Do not Whipstitch; attach to B.

A – Back
(cut 8) 23 x 23 holes
Overcast blue pieces.

Whipstitch to front.

Tab →

Whipstitch to front and back.

Whipstitch to front.

Do not Whipstitch; attach to B.

SPRINGTIME FRESH

Peekaboo Bunny

Designed by Deborah Rivers

LEVEL OF DIFFICULTY: Average

SIZE:
16¼" x 17½".

MATERIALS:
Five sheets of 7-count plastic canvas; One white 3" pom-pom; Craft glue or glue gun; Worsted-weight or plastic canvas yarn (for amounts see Color Key).

CUTTING INSTRUCTIONS:
NOTE: Graphs continued on pages 50 & 51.
A: For head front and backing, cut two (one for front and one for backing) according to graph.
B: For arm fronts and backings, cut four (two for fronts and two for backings) according to graph.
C: For foot #1 and foot #2 fronts and backings, cut two each (one each for fronts and one each for backings) according to graphs.
D: For legs front and backing, cut two (one for front and one for backing) according to graph.
E: For pockets, cut two according to graph.

STITCHING INSTRUCTIONS:
NOTE: Backing A-D pieces are not worked.
1: For fronts and pockets, using colors and stitches indicated (leave ¾" loops on Modified Turkey Work stitches), work one A, one of each C, one D and E pieces according to graphs; fill in uncoded areas of A and C pieces and work two B pieces on opposite sides of canvas using white and Continental Stitch. Fill in uncoded areas of front D using bt. green and Continental Stitch.

2: With yellow, Overcast edges of E pieces. Using black and Straight Stitch, embroider eyelashes on front A as indicated on graph. With matching colors, Whipstitch corresponding fronts and backings together.

3: Glue pieces together and pom-pom to Bunny as shown in photo.

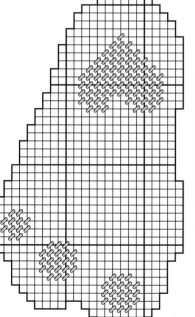

C – Foot #1
Front & Backing
(cut 1 each)
25 x 41 holes

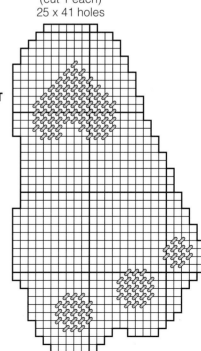

C – Foot #2
Front & Backing
(cut 1 each)
25 x 41 holes

COLOR KEY: Peekaboo Bunny

Worsted-weight	Nylon Plus™	Need-loft®	YARN AMOUNT
White	#01	#41	94 yds.
Bt. Green	–	#61	65 yds.
Pink	#11	#07	17 yds.
Yellow	#26	#57	8 yds.
Dk. Green	#31	#27	5 yds.
Black	#02	#00	4 yds.
Lt. Pink	#10	#08	3 yds.
Dusty Rose	#52	#06	2 yds.
Sail Blue	#04	#35	2 yds.

STITCH KEY:
— Straight Stitch
⌁ Modified Turkey Work

Peekaboo Bunny

Instructions & photo on pages 48 & 49

A – Head Front & Backing
(cut 1 each)
36 x 90 holes

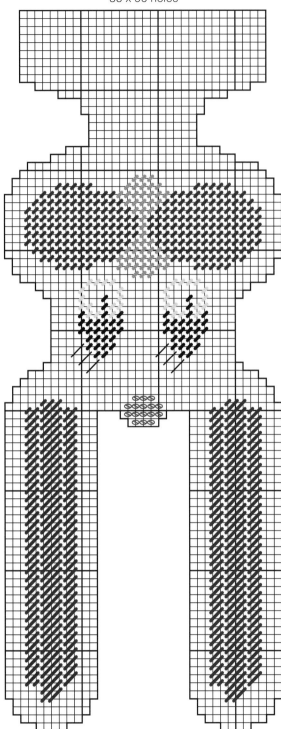

B – Arm
Front & Backing
(cut 2 each)
21 x 57 holes

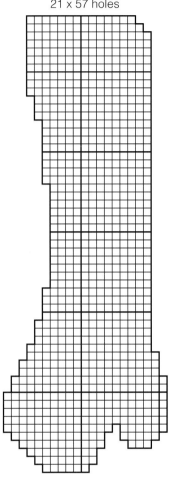

COLOR KEY: Peekaboo Bunny

	Worsted-weight	Nylon Plus™	Need-loft®	YARN AMOUNT
■	White	#01	#41	94 yds.
□	Bt. Green	–	#61	65 yds.
■	Pink	#11	#07	17 yds.
▨	Yellow	#26	#57	8 yds.
▨	Dk. Green	#31	#27	5 yds.
■	Black	#02	#00	4 yds.
▨	Lt. Pink	#10	#08	3 yds.
▨	Dusty Rose	#52	#06	2 yds.
▨	Sail Blue	#04	#35	2 yds.

STITCH KEY:

— Straight Stitch

⬭ Modified Turkey Work

E – Pocket
(cut 2)
12 x 13 holes

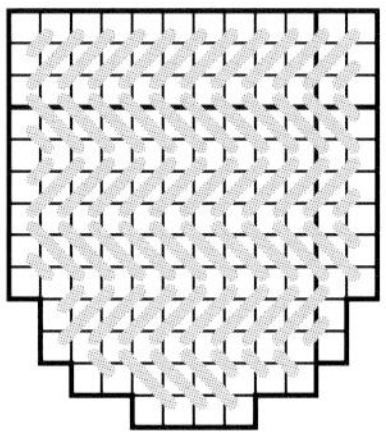

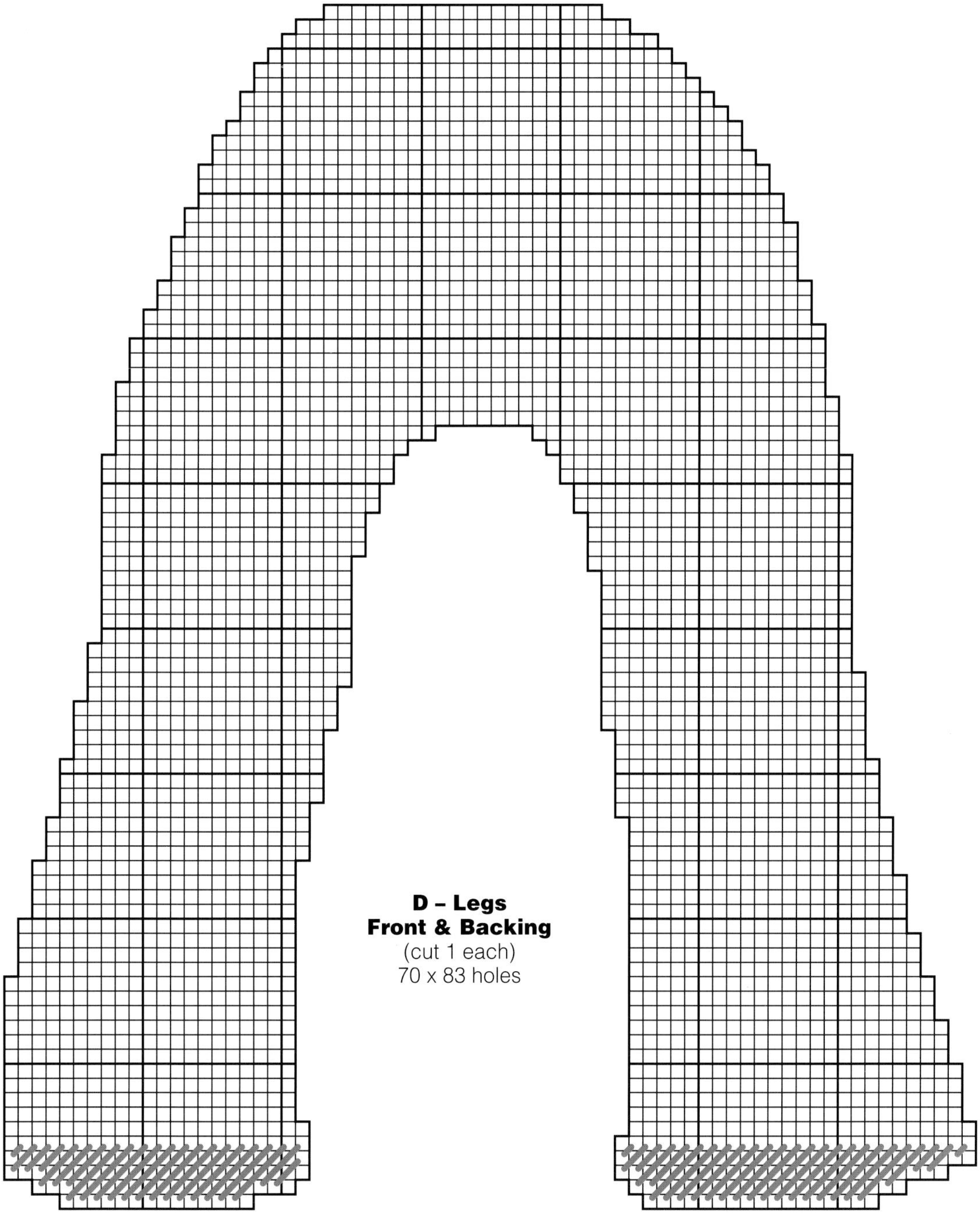

**D – Legs
Front & Backing**
(cut 1 each)
70 x 83 holes

SPRINGTIME FRESH

Spring Swing

Designed by Lynne L. Langer

LEVEL OF DIFFICULTY: Average

SIZE:
3¾" x 5¾" x 5¾" tall.

MATERIALS:
One sheet of clear and ¼ sheet each of ivory and lt. green 7-count plastic canvas; One 2" chenille chick with hat; Three small lavender silk flowers; Craft glue or glue gun; Six-strand embroidery floss (for amount see Color Key); Worsted-weight or plastic canvas yarn (for amounts see Color Key).

CUTTING INSTRUCTIONS:
A: For block sides, cut sixty-six from clear 5 x 5 holes (no graph).
B: For arch, cut two from ivory 5 x 73 holes.
C: For swing seat, cut one from ivory 5 x 12 holes.
D: For swing ropes, cut two from ivory 1 x 19 holes.
E: For base, cut one from lt. green 24 x 37 holes.

STITCHING INSTRUCTIONS:
NOTE: E piece is not worked.
1: Using lavender, lemon, lt. green and peach and Continental Stitch, work twelve A pieces in each color. Using lt. blue, pink and white and Continental Stitch, work six A pieces in each color.

2: Using six strands floss and Straight Stitch and alternating block side colors as desired or as shown in photo, embroider one letter centered on each of eleven A pieces as indicated on Letter Graph to spell greeting.

3: For each block, with desired contrasting color, Whipstitch one embroidered A and five matching solid color A pieces together.

4: For swing, with eggshell, Overcast edges of C, tacking one short end of each D piece to one end of C as indicated as you work;

do not Overcast edges of D pieces. Tack opposite ends of D pieces to one B as indicated and blocks to remaining B as indicated (see photo).

5: Holding B pieces wrong sides together (see photo), with eggshell, Whipstitch long edges together; with lt. green and working through all thicknesses to join, Whipstitch short ends of B pieces to E as indicated.

6: Glue flowers to arch and base and chick to swing seat as shown. ☺

Letter Graph

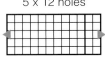

C – Swing Seat
(cut 1 from ivory)
5 x 12 holes

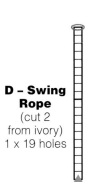

B – Arch
(cut 2 from ivory)
5 x 73 holes

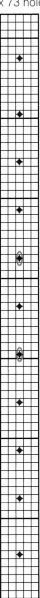

D – Swing Rope
(cut 2 from ivory)
1 x 19 holes

COLOR KEY: Spring Swing

Embroidery floss			AMOUNT
■ Black			4 yds.

Worsted-weight	Nylon Plus™	Need-loft®	YARN AMOUNT
☐ Lavender	#22	#45	5 yds.
☐ Lemon	#25	#20	5 yds.
☐ Lt. Green	#28	#26	5 yds.
☐ Peach	#46	#47	5 yds.
☐ Eggshell	#24	#39	4 yds.
☐ Lt. Blue	#05	#36	4 yds.
☐ Pink	#11	#07	3 yds.
☐ White	#01	#41	2 yds.

STITCH KEY:
- — Backstitch/Straight Stitch
- ▲ Swing Seat Attachment
- ◯ Swing Rope Attachment
- ✦ Block Attachment
- ☐ Arch Attachment

E – Base
(cut 1 from lt. green) 24 x 37 holes

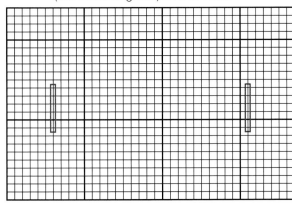

Mr. & Mrs. Hop

Designed by Barbara Tipton

LEVEL OF DIFFICULTY: Challenging

SIZE:
10½" x 28½" tall.

MATERIALS:
Two Uniek® Crafts 5" plastic canvas heart shapes; One sheet of 7-count plastic canvas; Two 13-mm round and two 13- x 18-mm oval blue faceted acrylic stones; 19 pink 6-mm faceted beads; Beading needle; Two of each pink and blue small silk roses; Eight pink small silk flowers; ⅓ yd. of 18-gauge wire; 7" white 2" lace; 9" lt. blue 1" lace; 4" red ¼" satin ribbon; 15" red dot ¾" grosgrain ribbon; 2 yds. pastel plaid 2½" stiff ribbon; Pink sewing thread; Two sheets of white and small amount of black felt; Aluminum foil; Craft glue and glue gun; #3 pearl cotton or six-strand embroidery floss (for amount see Color Key on page 56); Metallic cord (for amount see Color Key); Worsted-weight or plastic canvas yarn (for amounts see Color Key).

CUTTING INSTRUCTIONS:
NOTE: Graphs on page 56.
A: For heads, use heart shapes.
B: For Mr. Hop's ears, cut two according to graph.
C: For Mrs. Hop's right ear, cut one according to graph.
D: For Mrs. Hop's left ear, cut one according to graph.
E: For Mrs. Hop's left ear tip, cut one according to graph.
F: For hat front, cut one according to graph.
G: For hat crown, cut one according to graph.
H: For hat brim, cut one according to graph.
I: For hat back, cut one 12 x 16 holes (no graph).

STITCHING INSTRUCTIONS:
NOTE: I piece is not worked.

1: Using colors and stitches indicated, work A-H pieces according to graphs; fill in uncoded areas of A-E pieces using white and Continental Stitch.

2: With white, Overcast edges of A-C pieces. Holding wrong side of E to right side of D, with white, Whipstitch pieces together as indicated on graphs; Overcast unfinished edges.

3: Using #3 pearl cotton or six strands floss and Straight Stitch, embroider eyebrows, nose and mouth detail on one A for Mr. Hop's face and embroider nose and mouth detail only on remaining A for Mrs. Hop's face as indicated on graph.

4: For hat, with cord, Whipstitch F-I pieces together according to Hat Assembly Diagram on page 54; Overcast unfinished edges of brim.

NOTE: Cut one 12" length and one 6" length of pearl cotton or six-strand floss.

5: Stiffen cut pieces with craft glue; place 12" piece in a straight line and 6" piece in a circle on foil and let dry. For whiskers, cut 12" piece into 1" lengths. For eyelashes, cut 6" piece into ½" lengths.

6: Insert whiskers from front to back through ▲ holes on A pieces as indicated; glue at back to secure. Glue six eyelashes and oval stones to Mrs. Hop's face as shown in photo; glue remaining eyelashes and round stones to Mr. Hop's face as shown.

NOTE: Cut four 3" lengths of wire.

7: Glue ears to corresponding heads as shown; glue one length of wire to back of each ear for support. For Mrs. Hop's hat, gather white lace to form half circle and blue lace to form circle; glue lace and silk flowers (**NOTE:** Set two small pink flowers aside for Mr. Hop's hat.) together and to Mrs. Hop's head (see photo).

NOTE: Cut one 4" and one 5" length of pink thread.

8: For necklaces, with beading needle, thread eight pink beads on 4" piece and 11 beads on 5" pieces of thread. Glue ends of necklaces to back of Mrs. Hop's head as shown.

NOTES: Using heads and ear assemblies as patterns (Omit ear tip E when cutting pattern.), cut one each from white felt 1/8" smaller at all edges. Using hat back I as a pattern, cut one from black felt 1/8" smaller at all edges.

9: Glue felt backings to wrong side of corresponding pieces. Glue remaining small flowers to hat front; wrap red ribbon around hat as shown and glue ends at back to secure. Glue hat to Mr. Hop's head as shown.

NOTES: Cut red dot ribbon into one 2", one 6" and one 7" length. Cut plaid ribbon into one 4", one 19" and one 21" length; for hanger, trim one end of remaining plaid ribbon into a point (see photo).

10: Assemble plaid and red dot ribbon lengths into bows according to Bow Assembly diagram. Glue plaid bow to straight end of plaid hanger as shown. Glue heads and red dot bow to plaid hanger as shown. Hang as desired. :)

Bow Assembly Diagram
Step 1:
Fold each 6" and 7" red dot ribbons and each 19" and 21" plaid ribbons to form bow loops.

7" Red Dot or 21" Plaid Ribbon

6" Red Dot or 19" Plaid Ribbon

Step 2:
Fold each 2" red dot and 4" plaid ribbons lengthwise and crease, forming band.

2" Red Dot or 4" Plaid Ribbon

Step 3:
Wrap one band around corresponding bow loops; glue ends of band at back to secure.

Mr. & Mrs. Hop

Instructions & photo on pages 54 & 55

H – Hat Brim
(cut 1) 6 x 20 holes

Whipstitch to F.

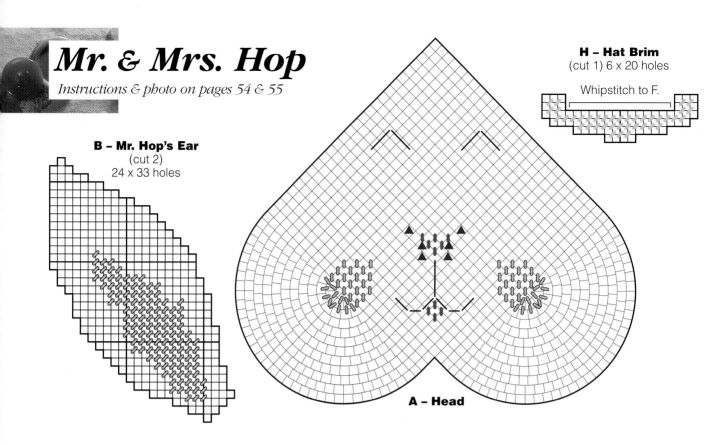

B – Mr. Hop's Ear
(cut 2)
24 x 33 holes

A – Head

G – Hat Crown
(cut 1)
9 x 12 holes

Hat Assembly Diagram

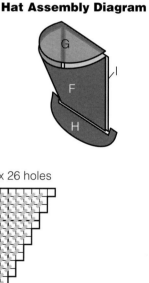

C – Mrs. Hop's Right Ear
(cut 1)
24 x 33 holes

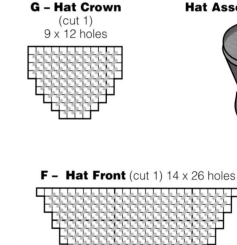

F – Hat Front (cut 1) 14 x 26 holes

D – Mrs. Hop's Left Ear
(cut 1) 22 x 22 holes
Whipstitch to E.

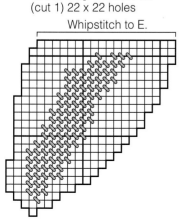

E – Mrs. Hop's Left Ear Tip
(cut 1) 13 x 18 holes
Whipstitch to D.

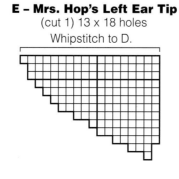

COLOR KEY: Mr. & Mrs. Hop

#3 pearl cotton or floss			AMOUNT
■ Black			2 yds.
Metallic cord			**AMOUNT**
▨ Black			9 yds.

Worsted-weight	Nylon Plus™	Need-loft®	YARN AMOUNT
□ White	#01	#41	61 yds.
▨ Lt. Pink	#10	#08	12 yds.
▨ Pink	#11	#07	1 yd.

STITCH KEY:
— Backstitch/Straight Stitch
▲ Whisker Placement

56

Poppy Poke
Instructions on page 58

Purple Passion

SPRINGTIME FRESH

Purple Passion

Designed by Brenda Wendling

LEVEL OF DIFFICULTY: Easy

SIZE:
Fridgie is 3" x 3";
Sachet is ¾" x 3" x 3⅛".

MATERIALS:
Three 3" plastic canvas heart shapes; Scrap of 7-count plastic canvas; One pearl shell stone; ½ cup of potpourri; ⅓ yd. white ¼" satin ribbon; Magnetic strip; ¾ yd. white pearlized metallic cord; Craft glue or glue gun; 1"-wide tulle (for amounts see Color Key on page 58); Worsted-weight or plastic canvas yarn (for amount see Color Key).

CUTTING INSTRUCTIONS:
NOTE: Graphs on page 58.
A: For Fridgie, use one heart shape.
B: For Sachet front and back, use two heart shapes (one for front and one for back).
C: For Sachet sides, cut two 4 x 31 holes.

STITCHING INSTRUCTIONS:
1: Using colors and stitches indicated, work pieces according to graphs. With purple, Overcast edges of A.

2: Holding C pieces wrong sides together, with purple, Whipstitch short edges together. For hanger, thread ends of ribbon from front to back through one hole at center of one joined end of C pieces; knot ribbon ends together on wrong side to secure.

Continued on next page

Purple Passion
Continued from page 57

3: For Sachet, holding B pieces wrong sides together with C pieces between (place hanger at top of heart as shown in photo), with purple, Whipstitch together, inserting potpourri before closing.

NOTE: Cut white cord into three 9" lengths; cut white tulle in half.

4: For Fridgie, glue one cord strand around inner edge on front and magnetic strip to back of A. Glue remaining cord strands around Sachet front and back as shown. Tie white tulle pieces into a bow or bows as desired (see photo); glue bows to Fridgie and Sachet. Glue stone to center of bow on Sachet. ⊙

C – Sachet Side
(cut 2)
4 x 31 holes

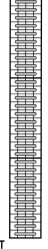

A – Fridgie

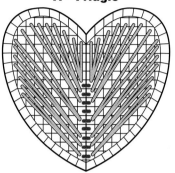

B – Sachet Front & Back

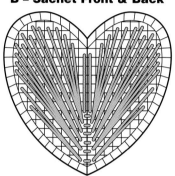

COLOR KEY: Purple Passion

1"-wide tulle			AMOUNT
▨ Lilac			3 yds.
☐ White			1 yd.

Worsted-weight	Nylon Plus™	Need-loft®	YARN AMOUNT
■ Purple	#21	#46	4 yds.

SPRINGTIME FRESH

Poppy Poke
Designed by Adele Mogavero

LEVEL OF DIFFICULTY: Easy

SIZE:
5" across x 10½" long, including stem.

MATERIALS:
½ sheet of 7-count plastic canvas; 1½" yellow pom-pom; 12" wooden ³⁄₁₆" dowel; ½ yd. green ¼" satin ribbon; Craft glue or glue gun; Worsted-weight or plastic canvas yarn (for amounts see Color Key).

CUTTING INSTRUCTIONS:
A: For petals, cut five according to graph.

STITCHING INSTRUCTIONS:
1: Using lavender and stitches indicated, work pieces according to graph; with lemon, Overcast edges.

2: Glue A pieces together according to Plant Poke Assembly Diagram; glue pom-pom to center front and dowel to back of petals (see diagram). Fold ribbon into a bow and glue to dowel as shown in photo. ⊙

A – Petal
(cut 5)
13 x 13 holes

Plant Poke Assembly Diagram

Pom-Pom

Dowel

COLOR KEY: Poppy Poke

Worsted-weight	Nylon Plus™	Need-loft®	YARN AMOUNT
■ Lavender	#22	#45	5 yds.
☐ Lemon	#25	#20	5 yds.

Basket of Chicks

Designed by Michele Wilcox

LEVEL OF DIFFICULTY: Easy

SIZE:
Each Coaster is 3¾" x 4¾".

MATERIALS:
One sheet of 7-count plastic canvas; One small round basket; #3 pearl cotton or six-strand embroidery floss (for amount see Color Key); Worsted-weight or plastic canvas yarn (for amounts see Color Key).

CUTTING INSTRUCTIONS:
A: For Coasters, cut four according to graph.

STITCHING INSTRUCTIONS:
1: Using colors indicated and Continental Stitch, work pieces according to graph; with matching colors, Overcast edges.

2: With #3 pearl cotton or six strands floss and French Knot, embroider eyes as indicated on graph. ☺

A – Coaster
(cut 4)
24 x 30 holes

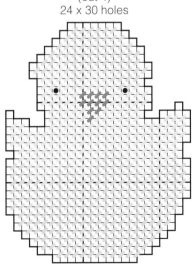

COLOR KEY: Basket of Chicks

#3 pearl cotton or floss			AMOUNT
■ Blue			1 yd.

Worsted-weight	Nylon Plus™	Need-loft®	YARN AMOUNT
☐ White	#01	#41	18 yds.
☐ Yellow	#26	#57	16 yds.
▨ Pumpkin	#50	#12	3 yds.

STITCH KEY:
● French Knot

59

Household Classics

Warm up a hearty dish for your new neighbors down the road, and take along a hand-stitched housewarming gift. And while you're getting to know one another, be sure to invite everyone to the weekly stitching circle on Auntie's old screened porch.

Victorian Fan

Designed by Glenda Chamberlain

LEVEL OF DIFFICULTY: Average

SIZE:
10½" x about 17", not including embellishments.

MATERIALS:
Three sheets of 10-count plastic canvas; 1 yd. each rose and pink and ½ yd. off-white ⅛" satin ribbon; ½ yd. each off-white and lt. blue ⅜" satin ribbon; ½ yd. lt. blue ¼" satin ribbon; 45 freshwater pearl beads; 15 gold 2-mm and five gold 5-mm beads; 3¾ yds. off-white ½" scallop-edge lace trim; 1 yd. pearl 2-mm bead string; #9 quilting needle or beading needle and off-white thread; Craft glue or glue gun; Six-strand embroidery floss (for amounts see Color Key on page 64).

CUTTING INSTRUCTIONS:
A: For blades and backings, cut ten (five for blades and five for backings) according to graph on page 64.

STITCHING INSTRUCTIONS:
NOTE: Five pieces are not worked for backings.

1: Using 12 strands in colors indicated and Continental Stitch, work five pieces for blades according to graph; fill in uncoded areas using ecru and Continental Stitch.

2: Using six strands lt. blue and Straight Stitch, embroider lattice detail (work cross-wise stitches above and below in a weaving pattern) as indicated on graph.

3: String and secure beads and freshwater pearls as indicated and according to Bead Attachment Diagram.

4: For each blade, holding one unworked piece to wrong side of one worked piece, with 12 strands blue, Whipstitch together.

5: Cutting lace to fit, glue straight edge of lace around outside edge on wrong side of each blade.

NOTE: Cut pearl bead string in half.

6: Holding ribbons, pearl strands and remaining lace together, tie into a knot at center. Stack blades with cutouts aligned. Thread one lt. blue ¼" ribbon tail onto needle; leaving embellishment knot to closely cover top cutout, run needle twice from top to bottom through cutouts of all blades. Tie threaded ribbon tail and its opposite end tail together in a tight knot against fan. ☺

Bead Attachment Diagram

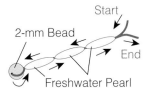

Start
End
2-mm Bead
Freshwater Pearl

Step 1:
For each bead string (make 15), with quilting or beading needle, run thread through three pearls and one 3-mm bead, back through pearls in reverse order; leave about 2" of thread hanging.

Step 2:
At indicated area on each blade, run thread tails of three bead strings from front to back through canvas; knot ends together against canvas on wrong side.

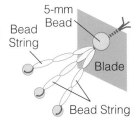

5-mm Bead
Bead String
Blade
Bead String

Step 3:
Sew one 5-mm bead to canvas; knot ends together against canvas on wrong side.

Victorian Fan
Instructions & photo on pages 62 & 63

A – Blade & Backing
(cut 5 each) 41 x 96 holes

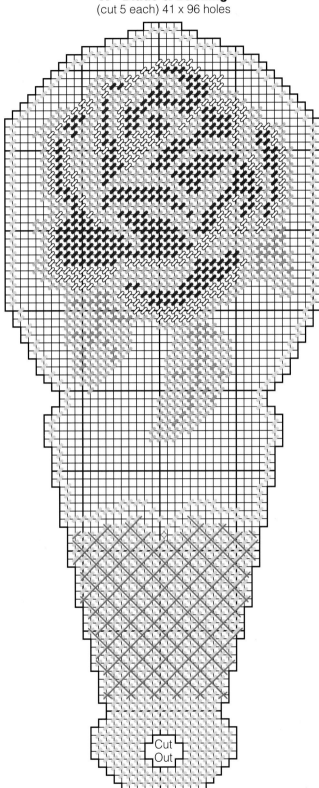

COLOR KEY: Victorian Fan

	Embroidery floss	AMOUNT
	Med. Blue	230 yds.
	Ecru	120 yds.
	Rose	70 yds.
	Scarlet	70 yds.
	Pink	50 yds.
	Fern	35 yds.
	Dk. Green	30 yds.
	Lt. Blue	28 yds.

STITCH KEY:

– Backstitch/Straight Stitch
◇ Pearl/Bead Attachment

Star of David

Designed by Jessi-ann Rosenbaum

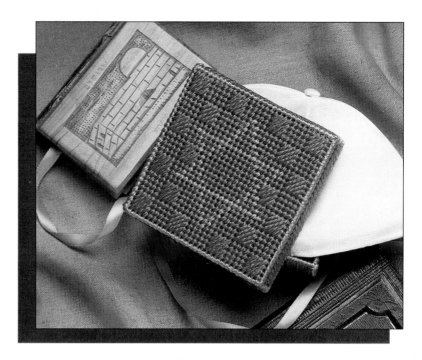

LEVEL OF DIFFICULTY: Average

SIZE:
4½" x 4¾" x 2½" tall.

MATERIALS FOR ONE:
One sheet of 7-count plastic canvas; Worsted-weight or plastic canvas yarn (for amounts see Color Key).

CUTTING INSTRUCTIONS:
A: For lid top, cut one 29 x 30 holes.
B: For lid sides, cut two 5 x 29 holes and two 5 x 30 holes (no graphs).
C: For box bottom, cut one 27 x 28 holes (no graph).
D: For box sides, cut two 15 x 27 holes and two 15 x 28 holes (no graphs).

STITCHING INSTRUCTIONS:
NOTE: C piece is not worked.

1: Using colors and stitches indicated, work A, B and D pieces according to graph and stitch pattern guides.

2: With lt. color, Whipstitch A and B pieces together, forming lid; Whipstitch C and D pieces together, forming box. Overcast edges of lid and box. ⊙

COLOR KEY: Star of David

Worsted-weight	YARN AMOUNT
■ Dk. Color	28 yds.
☐ Lt. Color	7 yds.

Box Side Stitch Pattern Guide

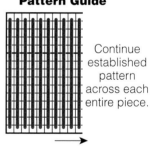

Continue established pattern across each entire piece.

Lid Side Stitch Pattern Guide

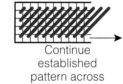

Continue established pattern across each entire piece.

A – Lid Top (cut 1) 29 x 30 holes

Fresh Veggies

Designed by Carol Nartowicz

LEVEL OF DIFFICULTY: Challenging

SIZE:
Coffee Box is 5¾" x 11¾" x 7¼" tall and holds filters and a 1-pound coffee can, or without divider holds napkins or mail; Towel Holder is 6¼" x 6⅜" x 6⅝" tall and holds a standard-size roll of paper towels; Corn Doorstop is 3⅜" x 7⅛" x 6¼" tall.

MATERIALS:
9½ sheets of 7-count plastic canvas; ¼ sheet of 14-count plastic canvas; 5½" x 11⅛" piece of iron-on fusable fleece (optional); Sewing needle and monofilament fishing line; Plastic spool-type paper towel holder; Zip-close bag filled with gravel or other weighting material; Paint brush; Repositionable glue; Craft glue or glue gun; Six-strand embroidery floss (for amounts see Corn Doorstop Color Key on page 79); Worsted-weight or plastic canvas yarn (for amounts see individual Color Keys on pages 69, 76 & 79).

COFFEE BOX

CUTTING INSTRUCTIONS:
NOTE: Graphs on pages 68 & 69.
A: For lid front and front lining, cut two (one for front and one for lining) according to graph.
B: For lid top, cut one 36 x 76 holes (no graph).
C: For lid ends, cut two 16 x 36 holes (no graph).
D: For box front and back, cut two (one for front and one for back) 37 x 74 holes (no graph).
E: For box ends, cut two 35 x 37 holes (no graph).
F: For box bottom, cut one 35 x 74 holes (no graph).
G: For box divider, cut one 34 x 36 holes (no graph).
H: For cabbage, cut two small, two medium and two large pieces according to graphs.
I: For cabbage inner leaves, cut three according to graph.
J: For cabbage outer leaves, cut four according to graph.
K: For tomatoes, cut four small, four medium and four large pieces according to graphs.
L: For tomato stems, cut two according to graph.
M: For corn ears, cut six small, six medium and

Continued on next page

Fresh Veggies

Continued from page 67

six large pieces according to graphs.

N: For long corn husks, cut five according to graph.

O: For short corn husk, cut one according to graph.

P: For carrot pieces, cut twelve according to graph.

STITCHING INSTRUCTIONS:

NOTE: Lining A, front D, F and G pieces are not worked.

1: Using colors and stitches indicated, work front A according to graph (leave indicated attachment areas unworked), and work B, C, back D and E pieces according to Coffee Box Stitch Pattern Guide.

NOTE: Paint each H, K and M piece with a thin layer of repositionable glue; let dry.

2: For cabbage, stacking H pieces as indicated on graph and working over and through all thicknesses as one piece, using lt. aqua and stitches indicated, work according to graph.

3: To attach cabbage, holding assembly to lid front A as indicated and reversing angle of stitches on graph, work stitches over assembly and through lid front A.

4: For each tomato (make two), stacking two of each K as indicated and working as for cabbage in Step 2, using red and stitches indicated, work according to graph; to attach each tomato, work stitches over assembly and through lid front A as for cabbage in Step 3.

5: For each corn ear (make three), stacking two

Continued on page 76

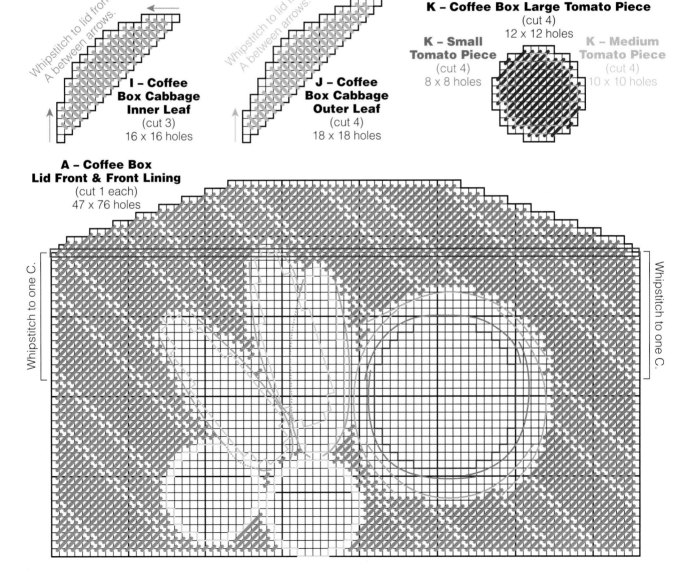

I – Coffee Box Cabbage Inner Leaf
(cut 3)
16 x 16 holes

Whipstitch to lid front A between arrows.

J – Coffee Box Cabbage Outer Leaf
(cut 4)
18 x 18 holes

Whipstitch to lid front A between arrows.

K – Coffee Box Large Tomato Piece
(cut 4)
12 x 12 holes

K – Small Tomato Piece
(cut 4)
8 x 8 holes

K – Medium Tomato Piece
(cut 4)
10 x 10 holes

A – Coffee Box Lid Front & Front Lining
(cut 1 each)
47 x 76 holes

Whipstitch to one C.

Whipstitch to one C.

I – Coffee Box Large Corn Ear
(cut 6)
7 x 23 holes

M – Small Corn Ear
(cut 6)
3 x 16 holes

M – Medium Corn Ear
(cut 6)
5 x 19 holes

N – Coffee Box Long Corn Husk
(cut 5)
4 x 23 holes

Whipstitch to lid front A between arrows.

O – Coffee Box Short Corn Husk
(cut 1)
4 x 14 holes

Whipstitch to front lid A between arrows.

P – Coffee Box Carrot Piece
(cut 12)
3 x 14 holes

Coffee Box Corn Ear Second Stitch Pattern

L – Coffee Box Tomato Stem
(cut 2)
7 x 10 holes

H – Coffee Box Large Cabbage Piece
(cut 2)
18 x 18 holes

H – Small Cabbage Piece
(cut 2)
14 x 14 holes

H – Medium Cabbage Piece
(cut 2)
16 x 16 holes

Coffee Box Stitch Pattern Guide

Continue established pattern up and across each entire piece.

COLOR KEY: Coffee Box

	Worsted-weight	Nylon Plus™	Need-loft®	YARN AMOUNT
	Tan	#33	#18	3¹/₂ oz.
	Beige	#43	#40	17 yds.
	Mint	#30	#24	14 yds.
	Lt. Aqua	#39	#49	10 yds.
	Lt. Yellow	#42	#21	8 yds.
	Red	#19	#02	8 yds.
	Moss	#48	#25	5 yds.
	Orange	#17	#58	5 yds.
	Straw	#41	#19	5 yds.
	Dk. Green	#31	#27	4 yds.
	Green	#58	#28	4 yds.

STITCH KEY:

☐ Cabbage Attachment
☐ Tomato Attachment
☐ Corn Ear Attachment
○ Lark's Head Knot/Carrot Top Attachment
— Inner Cabbage Leaf Attachment
— Outer Cabbage Leaf Attachment
— Long Corn Husk Attachment
— Short Corn Husk Attachment
☐ Lid Lining/Top Attachment

Coffee Box Assembly Diagram
(Wrong sides shown in gray; unworked pieces shown in eggshell.)

Step 1:
Whipstitch one long edge of G to front D; tack opposite edge of G to back D, forming divider assembly.

Back D
G
Front D
34 Holes
40 Holes

Step 2:
Whipstitch divider assembly, E and F pieces together, forming box assembly.

E
E
F

Step 3:
Omitting end/lining edges, Whipstitch lining A, B and C pieces together; Whipstitch B to box assembly.

Lining A
C
B
C
Box Assembly

B
C
Front A
Lining A

Step 4:
(Vegetables not shown.)
Whipstitch A pieces and lid ends together.

69

HOUSEHOLD CLASSICS

Game Time

Designed by Celia Lange Designs

LEVEL OF DIFFICULTY: Average

SIZE:
Each Coaster is 3½" square;
Coaster Holder is 1⅜" x 3⅞" x 1⅞" tall;
Card Box is 1⅜" x 4⅜" x 6½".

MATERIALS:
Two sheets of 7-count plastic canvas; One beige 9" x 12" sheet of felt; Sewing needle and crimson thread; Craft glue or glue gun; Worsted-weight or plastic canvas yarn (for amounts see Color Key).

CUTTING INSTRUCTIONS:
A: For Coasters, cut four 23 x 23 holes.
B: For Holder front, cut one according to graph.

C: For Holder back, cut one 11 x 25 holes.
D: For Holder ends, cut two 8 x 11 holes.
E: For Holder bottom, cut one 8 x 25 holes (no graph).
F: For Card Box outside and inside lid pieces, cut two (one for outside and one for inside) 28 x 42 holes.
G: For Card Box sides, cut two 8 x 42 holes (no graph).
H: For Card Box ends, cut two 8 x 28 holes (no graph).
I: For Card Box bottom, cut one 28 x 42 holes (no graph).
J: For Card Box divider pieces, cut two 5 x 26 holes (no graph).
K: For Coaster and Holder linings, using A-E pieces as patterns, cut one each from felt ⅛" smaller at all edges.
L: For Card Box linings, using G-I pieces as patterns, cut one each from felt ⅛" smaller at all edges.

70

STITCHING INSTRUCTIONS:

NOTE: Use a double strand for Whipstitch and Overcast.

1: Using colors and stitches indicated, work A–D (reverse pattern on one end) and F–H pieces according to graphs and stitch pattern guide; fill in uncoded areas using eggshell and Continental Stitch. Using violet and Cross Stitch, work E and I pieces; using crimson and Continental Stitch, work J pieces.

2: Glue K and L pieces to wrong side of corresponding pieces.

3: For Coasters and Holder, with crimson, Whipstitch B–E pieces together according to Holder Assembly Diagram; Overcast edges of A pieces and Holder.

4: For Card Box, with crimson, Whipstitch G–I pieces together according to Card Box Assembly Diagram; Overcast edges. For lid, holding F pieces wrong sides together, Whipstitch together; for divider, holding J pieces wrong sides together, Whipstitch together.

5: Glue divider to inside of Card Box (see diagram). With thread, sew one long edge of lid to one side of box.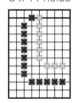

A – Coaster
(cut 4) 23 x 23 holes

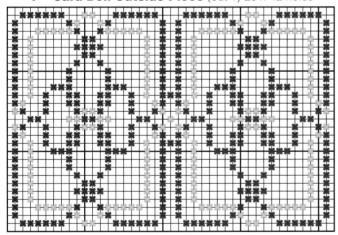

B – Holder Front
(cut 1)
11 x 25 holes

C – Holder Back
(cut 1) 11 x 25 holes

F – Card Box Outside Piece (cut 1) 28 x 42 holes

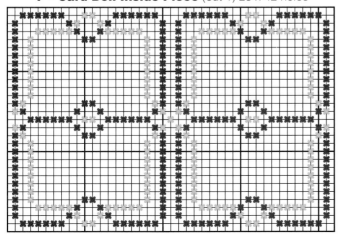

D – Holder End
(cut 2)
8 x 11 holes

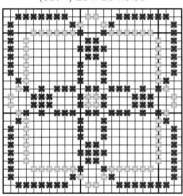

Card Box Side & End Stitch Pattern Guide

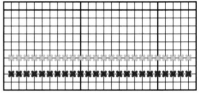

Continue established →
pattern across each
entire piece.

F – Card Box Inside Piece (cut 1) 28 x 42 holes

COLOR KEY: Game Time

	Worsted-weight	Nylon Plus™	Need-loft®	YARN AMOUNT
■ Violet	#49	#04	60 yds.
▨ Crimson	#53	#42	45 yds.
□ Eggshell	#24	#39	40 yds.

Holder Assembly Diagram

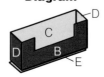

Card Box Assembly Diagram

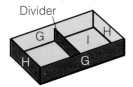

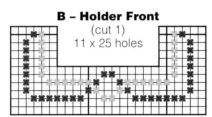

Amethyst Treasures

Designed by Karin L. Laflin

LEVEL OF DIFFICULTY: Challenging

SIZE:
Tissue Cover loosely covers a boutique-style tissue box; Bathroom Tissue Cover hides a standard-size roll of bathroom tissue; Large Trinket Box is 4¾" across x 3" tall, not including handle; Small Trinket Box is 3½" across x 2¼" tall; Ring Box is 2⅛" across x 1½" tall.

MATERIALS:
Three 12" x 18" or larger sheets of stiff 7-count plastic canvas; Ten 3" Darice®, four 4¼" and two 6" plastic canvas radial circles; One 20-mm, one 18-mm and four 15-mm dk. amethyst half-round foil-backed acrylic stones; Velcro® closure (optional); #9 quilting needle or beading needle; Monofilament fishing line; Clear-drying craft glue; Pearls and beads (for amounts see Beading Key on page 75); Metallic cord (for amount see Color Key on page 75); 3-ply wool yarn (for amount see Color Key).

WOOL PREPARATION INSTRUCTIONS:
1: Untwist wool from packages; cut into 36" lengths.

2: Separate each length into single plies by holding two plies firmly and pulling out the third. Let each ply untwist naturally; drape strands over chair arm to hold during stitching.

3: For 3-ply stitches (see Color Key), hold three separated strands together. For 2-ply stitches, hold two separated strands together. For single-ply stitches, use one strand alone.

TISSUE COVERS

CUTTING INSTRUCTIONS:
NOTE: Graphs on page 75.

A: For Tissue Cover top, cut one according to graph.
B: For Tissue Cover sides, cut four 31 x 37 holes.
C: For optional Tissue Cover bottom and flap, cut one 31 x 31 holes for bottom and one 12 x 31 holes for flap (no graphs).
D: For Bathroom Tissue Cover side, cut one 31 x 103 holes (no graph).
E: For Bathroom Tissue Cover top and lining, cut away outer three rows of holes from one 6" circle for top and outer four rows of holes from remaining 6" circle for lining (no lining graph).
F: For Bathroom Tissue Cover handle pieces, cut away outer four rows of holes from two 3" circles (no graph).

STITCHING INSTRUCTIONS:
NOTE: Lining E and C pieces are not worked.
1: Overlapping two holes as indicated on Bathroom Tissue Cover Side Stitch Pattern Guide on page 75, with fishing line, sew ends of D together, forming cylinder. Using cord and Continental Stitch, work A, B and D pieces according to graphs and stitch pattern guide; using 3-, 2- and single-ply wool strands, Cross Stitch, Herringbone Stitch, Sheaf Stitch and stitches indicated, work remainder of A, B and D (hide yarn ends under cord stitches) and work top E and F pieces according to graphs and stitch pattern guides; using cord and stitches indicated, work remainder of top E according to stitch pattern guide.

2: With fishing line, sew beads and pearls to pieces as indicated on graphs and stitch pattern guides.

3: For handle, holding F pieces wrong sides together, with cord, Whipstitch together; tack one edge of handle tightly to center of top E (see photo). Using fishing line and Running Stitch, sew lining E to center on wrong side of top E. Glue one 18-mm stone to each side of handle (see photo).

Continued on page 74

4: For Tissue Cover, with cord, Overcast cutout edges of A; Whipstitch A and B pieces together. For optional bottom, Whipstitch C pieces together and to Cover according to Optional Tissue Cover Bottom Assembly Diagram; Overcast unfinished edges of Cover. If desired, glue closure to flap and inside of Cover.

5: For Bathroom Tissue Cover, with cord, Whipstitch D and E pieces together; Overcast bottom edge.

RING & TRINKET BOXES

CUTTING INSTRUCTIONS:

A: For Large Trinket Box side, cut one 15 x 90 holes (no graph).
B: For Large Trinket Box bottom, lid and lid lining, use 4¼" circles (no graphs).
C: For Large Trinket Box bottom lining, cut away one outer row of holes from one 4¼" circle (no graph).
D: For Large Trinket Box side lining, cut one 13 x 83 holes (no graph).
E: For Large Trinket Box lid lip, cut one 4 x 76 holes (no graph).
F: For Large Trinket Box handle pieces, cut away outer four rows of holes from two 3" circles (no graph).
G: For Small Trinket Box side, cut one 7 x 63 holes (no graph).
H: For Small Trinket Box bottom and lid, use 3" circles (no graphs).
I: For Small Trinket Box lid top motif, cut away outer five rows of holes from one 3" circle (no graph).
J: For Small Trinket Box lid side, cut one 3 x 62 holes (no graph).
K: For Small Trinket Box lid lining, cut away one outer row of holes from one 3" circle (no graph).
L: For Small Trinket Box lid lip, cut one 4 x 57 holes (no graph).
M: For Ring Box side, cut one 7 x 37 holes (no graph).
N: For Ring Box bottom and lid, cut away outer four rows of holes from remaining 3" circles (no graphs).
O: For Ring Box lid lip, cut one 1 x 30 holes (no graph).

STITCHING INSTRUCTIONS:

NOTE: Bottom and lid lining B, C-E, bottom H, K, L, bottom N and O pieces are not worked.
1: For each box side, overlapping two holes as indicated on side stitch pattern guides, with fishing line, sew ends of A, G and M together, forming cylinders. Using cord and Continental Stitch, work A, G and M pieces according to stitch pattern guides; using 3-, 2- and single-ply wool strands, Cross Stitch, Herringbone Stitch and Sheaf Stitch, work remainder of each piece (hide yarn ends under cord stitches), and work one B for lid according to Bathroom Tissue Cover Top Stitch Pattern Guide, F according to Bathroom Tissue Cover Handle Stitch Pattern Guide, one H for lid according to Small Trinket Box Lid Stitch Pattern Guide, I according to Small Trinket Box Lid Top Motif Stitch Pattern Guide, J (overlap two holes as indicated and work through both thicknesses at overlap area to join) according to Small Trinket Box & Ring Box Side Stitch Pattern Guide, and one N for lid according to Bathroom Tissue Cover Handle Stitch Pattern Guide.

2: With fishing line, sew beads and pearls to pieces as indicated on stitch pattern guides.

3: For Large Trinket Box handle, holding F pieces wrong sides together, with cord, Whipstitch together; tack one edge of handle tightly to center of lid B (see photo). Glue one 18-mm stone to each side of handle (see photo). For lid, overlapping two holes at ends of E, with fishing line, Whipstitch ends together; Whipstitch E centered on lid lining B at second hole from outside edge. Holding lid and lid lining B pieces together, with cord, Whipstitch together.

4: For Large Trinket Box, with cord, Whipstitch A and bottom B together; Overcast top edge. For lining, overlapping one hole at ends of D, with fishing line, Whipstitch together, forming cylinder; for lining, Whipstitch C and D together. Place lining inside box; with fishing line, tack lining to box to secure.

5: For Medium Trinket Box, with cord, Whipstitch G and bottom H together; Overcast top edge. For lid, Whipstitch lid H and J together; Overcast edges of J and I. For lid lining, overlapping three holes at ends of L, with fishing line, Whipstitch together; Whipstitch K and L together. With fishing line, Whipstitch lining to inside edge on wrong side of lid H. Glue I to center of lid and one 18-mm stone to center of I (see photo).

6: For Ring Box, with cord, Whipstitch M and bottom N together; Overcast top edge and edge of lid N. For lid lip, overlapping two holes at ends of O, with fishing line, Whipstitch together; Whipstitch O to wrong side center of lid N. Glue 20-mm stone to center of lid (see photo). ⊡

COLOR KEY: Amethyst Treasures

Metallic cord	AMOUNT
▨ White/Gold	81 yds.

3-ply wool	AMOUNT
☐ Off-white	3¹/₂ oz.
▨ 3 strands	
▨ 2 strands	
▨ 1 strand	

BEADING KEY:

6-mm	AMOUNT
○ Pearls	214
✦ Dk. Amethyst Beads	223
▲ Lt. Amethyst Beads	244

4-mm	AMOUNT
✪ Pearls	96

Small Trinket Box & Ring Box Side Stitch Pattern Guide

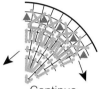

Lap Over

Continue established pattern around entire piece.

Small Trinket Box Lid Side Stitch Pattern Guide

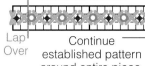

Lap Over

Continue established pattern around entire piece.

Small Trinket Box Lid Top Motif Stitch Pattern Guide

Continue established pattern around entire piece.

Small Trinket Box Lid Stitch Pattern Guide

Continue established pattern around entire piece.

Large Trinket Box Side Stitch Pattern Guide

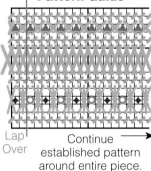

Lap Over

Continue established pattern around entire piece.

Bathroom Tissue Cover Top Stitch Pattern Guide

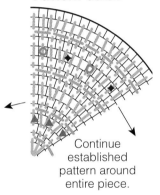

Continue established pattern around entire piece.

Bathroom Tissue Cover Handle Stitch Pattern Guide

Continue established pattern around entire piece.

Optional Tissue Cover Bottom Assembly Diagram

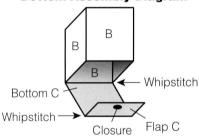

B

B

B

Whipstitch

Bottom C

Whipstitch

Closure

Flap C

B – Tissue Cover Side
(cut 4) 31 x 37 holes

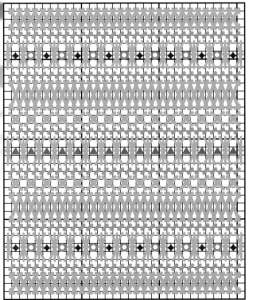

A – Tissue Cover Top
(cut 1) 31 x 31 holes

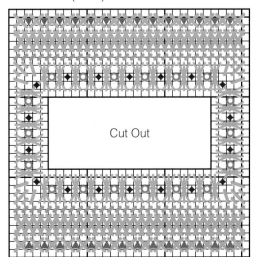

Cut Out

Bathroom Tissue Cover Side Stitch Pattern Guide

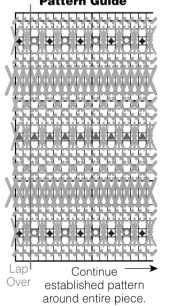

Lap Over

Continue established pattern around entire piece.

75

of each M as indicated and working as for cabbage in Step 2, using straw and stitches indicated, work according to graph; using lt. yellow and stitches indicated, work over stitches according to Corn Ear Second Stitch Pattern graph on page 69. To attach each corn ear, holding each assembly to lid front A as indicated, with lt. yellow, Whipstitch together.

6: Using colors and stitches indicated, work I, J, L, N (three on opposite side of canvas) and O pieces according to graphs; with matching colors, Overcast edges.

7: For each carrot, holding three P pieces together and working through all thickness as one piece, using orange and stitches indicated, work according to graph; Whipstitch edges together.

NOTE: Cut green yarn into 12 equal lengths.

8: For carrot tops, using one strand of green yarn, work a Lark's Head Knot in each indicated hole on each carrot; pull ends to even. Trim ends and separate plies with needle to fluff.

9: With fishing line, overlapping pieces as needed (see photo), sew I, J, N and O pieces to lid top A as indicated; tack overlapped pieces together.

10: For Coffee Box, with tan, Whipstitch A-G pieces together (If desired, hold fusable fleece to inside of front D and work through fleece to attach during assembly.) as indicated and according to Coffee Box Assembly Diagram on page 69; Overcast unfinished edges of Box.

11: With fishing line, tack or glue tomato stems and carrots to lid front as shown in photo.

TOWEL HOLDER

CUTTING INSTRUCTIONS:
A: For front and lining, cut two (one for front and one for lining) 40 x 40 holes.
B: For sides and linings, cut four (two for sides and two for linings) according to graph.
C: For base top, cut one according to graph.
D: For base bottom, cut one 40 x 40 holes (no graph).
E: For pumpkin base, cut one according to graph.
F: For pumpkin center pieces, cut two small, two medium and two large pieces according to graphs.
G: For pumpkin side pieces, cut four small and four large pieces according to graphs.
H: For pumpkin stem, cut one according to graph.
I: For leaves, cut two according to graph.

STITCHING INSTRUCTIONS:
NOTE: Lining A, lining B, C and D pieces are not worked.
1: Using colors and stitches indicated and omitting horizontal stitches on pumpkin, work front A,

Continued on page 78

A – Towel Holder Front & Lining
(cut 1 each) 40 x 40 holes

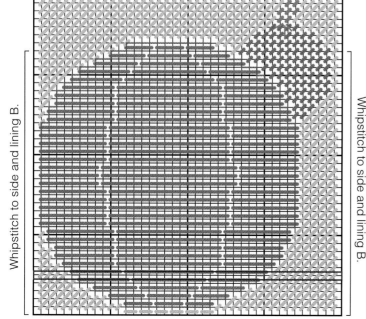

Whipstitch to side and lining B.

Whipstitch to side and lining B.

COLOR KEY: Towel Holder

	Worsted-weight	Nylon Plus™	Need-loft®	YARN AMOUNT
▨ Pumpkin		#50	#12	32 yds.
▨ Beige		#43	#40	24 yds.
▨ Cinnamon		#44	#14	3 yds.
▨ Forest		#32	#29	3 yds.
▢ Gold		#27	#17	3 yds.

STITCH KEY:
— Backstitch/Straight Stitch
▢ Pumpkin Large Piece Attachment
▢ Pumpkin Medium Piece Attachment
▢ Pumpkin Small Piece Attachment
▢ Pumpkin Base Attachment
▢ Front Lining/Base Top Attachment
▢ Side Lining/Base Top Attachment

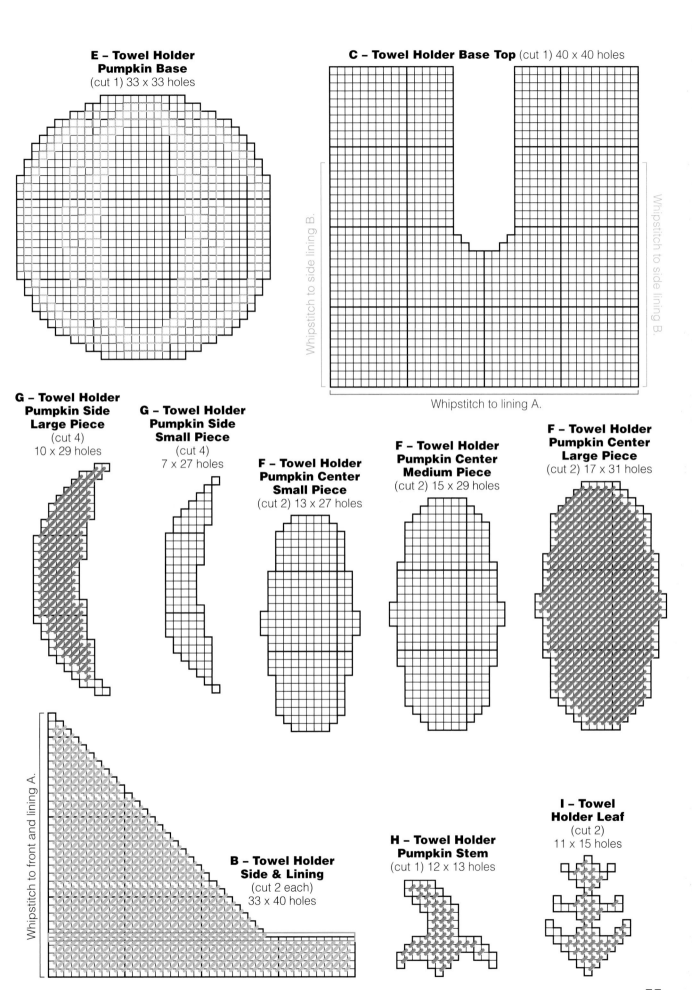

E – Towel Holder Pumpkin Base
(cut 1) 33 x 33 holes

C – Towel Holder Base Top (cut 1) 40 x 40 holes

Whipstitch to side lining B.

Whipstitch to side lining B.

Whipstitch to lining A.

G – Towel Holder Pumpkin Side Large Piece
(cut 4)
10 x 29 holes

G – Towel Holder Pumpkin Side Small Piece
(cut 4)
7 x 27 holes

F – Towel Holder Pumpkin Center Small Piece
(cut 2) 13 x 27 holes

F – Towel Holder Pumpkin Center Medium Piece
(cut 2) 15 x 29 holes

F – Towel Holder Pumpkin Center Large Piece
(cut 2) 17 x 31 holes

Whipstitch to front and lining A.

B – Towel Holder Side & Lining
(cut 2 each)
33 x 40 holes

H – Towel Holder Pumpkin Stem
(cut 1) 12 x 13 holes

I – Towel Holder Leaf
(cut 2)
11 x 15 holes

Fresh Veggies

Continued from page 76

Towel Holder Assembly Diagram. Glue pumpkin stem and leaves to front as shown in photo. One end of spool-type paper towel holder slides in slot on base top.

CORN DOORSTOP

CUTTING INSTRUCTIONS:
NOTE: Use 14-count canvas for G and H pieces.
A: For box sides, cut two 29 x 46 holes (no graph).
B: For box ends, cut two 21 x 29 holes (no graph).
C: For box insert, cut one 20 x 45 holes (no graph).
D: For box bottom, cut one 21 x 46 holes (no graph).
E: For corn ear small, medium and large pieces, cut eighteen each according to Coffee Box M graphs on page 69.
F: For corn husks, cut eighteen according to Coffee Box N graph.
G: For vegetable sign, cut one according to graph.
H: For corn signs, cut three according to graph.

STITCHING INSTRUCTIONS:
NOTE: D piece is not worked.
1: Using colors and stitches indicated, work A-C (leave indicated area on A and B pieces unworked) pieces according to stitch pattern guides; with cinnamon for insert attachment and bottom and with matching colors, Whipstitch A-D pieces together as indicated on stitch pattern guides and according to Doorstop Assembly Diagram. With beige, Overcast unfinished edges of box.

NOTE: Paint each E piece with a thin layer of repositionable glue; let dry.

2: For each corn ear (make nine), stacking two of each E as indicated and working over and through all thicknesses as one piece, using lt. yellow and stitches indicated, work according to graph; using colors and stitches indicated, work over stitches according to Corn Ear Second Stitch Pattern graph. With straw, Whipstitch unfinished edges together.

two B pieces (one on opposite side of canvas) for sides, H and one I piece according to graphs; substituting gold for cinnamon, work remaining I according to graph. With matching colors, Overcast edges of H and I pieces.

2: Using forest and Straight Stitch, embroider stem detail on front A as indicated on graph.

NOTE: Paint E and each F and G piece with a thin layer of repositionable glue; let dry.

3: Stacking F and G pieces on E as indicated and working over and through all thicknesses as one piece, using pumpkin and stitches indicated, work according to large F and G graphs. Holding E over front A as indicated, using pumpkin and stitches indicated, work stitches over assembly and through front A according to front A graph.

4: Whipstitch A-D pieces together according to

Towel Holder Assembly Diagram
(back view)

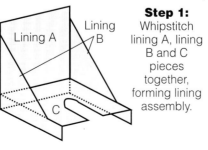

Step 1: Whipstitch lining A, lining B and C pieces together, forming lining assembly.

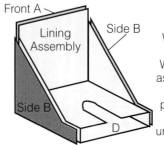

Step 2: With right sides facing out, Whipstitch lining assembly, front A, side B and D pieces together; Overcast unfinished edges.

3: Using mint and stitches indicated, work F pieces (nine on opposite side of canvas) according to graph; Overcast unfinished edges. With fishing line, sew two husks to each ear according to Husk Attachment Diagram.

4: Using six strands floss and stitches indicated, work G and H pieces according to graphs; with matching colors, Overcast edges. Using three strands floss in colors indicated, Backstitch and Straight Stitch, embroider signs as indicated.

5: Glue corn inside top and signs to outside of Doorstop as shown in photo. ☺

G – Doorstop Vegetable Sign
(cut 1 from 14 count) 20 x 43 holes

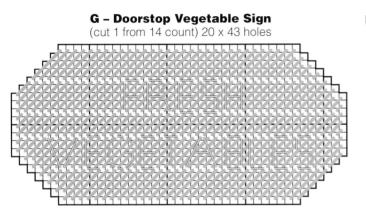

H – Doorstop Corn Sign
(cut 3 from 14-count) 9 x 18 holes

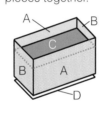

Doorstop Husk Attachment Diagram

Corn Ear

Corn Husk

COLOR KEY: Corn Doorstop

Embroidery floss			AMOUNT
Red			7 yds.
White			5 yds.

Worsted-weight	Nylon Plus™	Need-loft®	YARN AMOUNT
Beige	#43	#40	46 yds.
Lt. Yellow	#42	#21	35 yds.
Mint	#30	#24	26 yds.
Straw	#41	#19	20 yds.
Cinnamon	#44	#14	13 yds.
Green	#58	#28	11 yds.

STITCH KEY:
— Backstitch/Straight Stitch
☐ Unworked Area/Insert Attachment

Doorstop Insert Stitch Pattern Guide

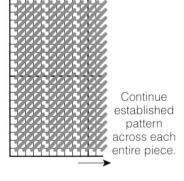

Continue established pattern across each entire piece.

Doorstop Assembly Diagram
Step 1:
Whipstitch A-C pieces together.

Step 2:
Whipstitch assembly and D together, inserting zip-close bag filled with weight before closing.

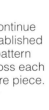

A
B
C
B
A
D

Doorstop Side and End Stitch Pattern Guide

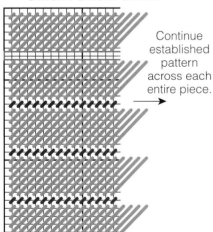

Continue established pattern across each entire piece.

Awesome Autumn

As the leaves turn a golden hue, gather a harvest of back-to-school goodies, and trick-or-treat your friends and family to a special, home-spun fall full of fun. Before the goblins arrive, catch the holiday spirit with Halloween projects the entire family will enjoy stitching together.

Apples for Teacher

Instructions on page 83

Teacher's Tissues

Designed by Debby Keel

LEVEL OF DIFFICULTY: Challenging

SIZE:
Loosely covers a boutique-style tissue box.

MATERIALS:
2½ sheets of 7-count plastic canvas; One gold 16-mm liberty bell; Eight assorted ½ - ¾" buttons; Two white 7-mm star stones; Velcro® closure (optional); Craft glue or glue gun; Worsted-weight or plastic canvas yarn (for amounts see Color Key).

CUTTING INSTRUCTIONS:
NOTE: Graphs continued on page 84.
A: For house front and back, cut two (one for front and one for back) according to graph.
B: For house sides, cut two 33 x 36 holes.
C: For optional cover bottom and flap, cut one 31 x 32 holes for bottom and one 12 x 31 holes for flap (no graphs).
D: For house roof sides #1 and #2, cut one each according to graphs.
E: For bell tower sides, cut four according to graph.
F: For bell tower ends, cut two 3 x 9 holes (no graph).
G: For bell tower roof sides, cut two 13 x 13 holes.

STITCHING INSTRUCTIONS:
NOTE: C pieces are not worked.
1: Using colors and stitches indicated, work one A for front, B, D, E and G pieces according to graphs. Using dk. red and Continental Stitch, work remaining A for back and F pieces.

2: Using colors indicated and Straight Stitch, embroider flower stems on B pieces and door detail on front A as indicated on graphs.

3: With dk. red, Whipstitch A and B pieces together as indicated; for optional bottom, Whipstitch C pieces together and to back A according to Optional Tissue Cover Bottom Assembly Diagram on page 103. Overcast unfinished edges of A-C pieces; if desired, glue closure to flap and inside of front A.

4: With black, Whipstitch D pieces wrong sides together as indicated, forming house roof; Overcast edges. Glue roof to top of house as shown in photo.

NOTE: Cut one 4" length of black.

5: For bell tower, with indicated and matching colors, Whipstitch and assemble E-G pieces, liberty bell and 4" black strand as indicated and according to Bell Tower Assembly Diagram on page 103. Glue bell tower to house roof as shown.

6: Glue buttons to house front and sides and one star stone to each side of roof as indicated (see photo). ⊛

COLOR KEY: Teacher's Tissues

	Worsted-weight	Nylon Plus™	Need-loft®	YARN AMOUNT
◼	Dk. Red	#20	#01	65 yds.
◼	Black	#02	#00	36 yds.
◻	White	#01	#41	16 yds.
◼	Denim	#06	#33	4 yds.
◻	Dusty Blue	#38	#34	4 yds.
◻	Mint	#30	#24	4 yds.
◼	Forest	#32	#29	1 yd.

STITCH KEY:
— Backstitch/Straight Stitch
○ Button Placement
✦ Star Stone Placement

E – Bell Tower Side
(cut 4)
17 x 19 holes

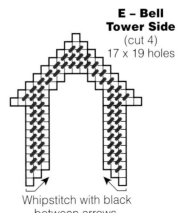

Whipstitch with black between arrows.

Teacher's Tissues

Instructions & photo on pages 82 & 83

A – Front & Back
(cut 1 each)
31 x 50 holes

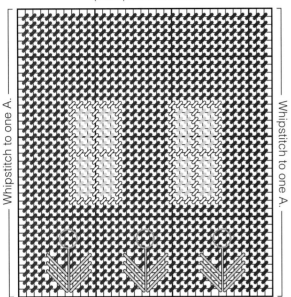

B – Side
(cut 2) 33 x 36 holes

Whipstitch to one A.

Whipstitch to one A.

Whipstitch to one B.

Whipstitch to one B.

D – House Roof Side #2 (cut 1) 25 x 41 holes

Whipstitch   Whipstitch

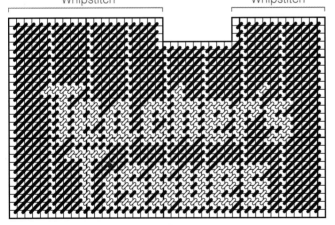

G – Bell Tower Roof Side
(cut 2) 13 x 13 holes

Whipstitch

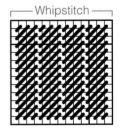

D – House Roof Side #1 (cut 1) 25 x 41 holes

Whipstitch   Whipstitch

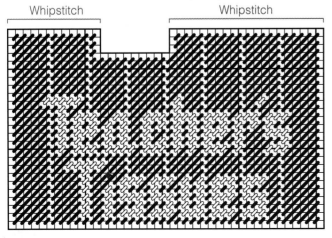

COLOR KEY: Teacher's Tissues

	Worsted-weight	Nylon Plus™	Need-loft®	YARN AMOUNT
■	Dk. Red	#20	#01	65 yds.
■	Black	#02	#00	36 yds.
▨	White	#01	#41	16 yds.
▨	Denim	#06	#33	4 yds.
▨	Dusty Blue	#38	#34	4 yds.
▨	Mint	#30	#24	4 yds.
▨	Forest	#32	#29	1 yd.

STITCH KEY:

— Backstitch/Straight Stitch

○ Button Placement

✦ Star Stone Placement

Apples for Teacher

Designed by Debby Keel

LEVEL OF DIFFICULTY: Easy

SIZE:
Bell Pull is 5½" across x 24½" long including ribbon and has two photo frames with 1¼"-square photo windows; Coaster is 3⅞" square.

MATERIALS FOR ONE OF EACH:
1½ sheets of 7-count plastic canvas; 1⅓ yds. red/white dotted 1" grosgrain ribbon; One gold 25-mm liberty bell; Craft glue or glue gun; Worsted-weight or plastic canvas yarn (for amounts see Color Key).

CUTTING INSTRUCTIONS:
A: For cutout squares, cut three according to graph.
B: For solid squares, cut five 25 x 25 holes.

STITCHING INSTRUCTIONS:
NOTE: One A and three B pieces are not worked.
1: Using colors and stitches indicated, work two A and two B pieces according to graphs.

2: For Bell Pull photo frame, glue photo to wrong side of one worked A; holding one unworked B to wrong side of worked A, with dk. red, Whipstitch together.

NOTE: Cut one 6" length of dk. red.

3: For Bell Pull bell frame, thread 6" strand through hole at top of bell; holding unworked A to wrong side of remaining worked A with ends of 6" strand between at one inner point (see photo on page 82), with black, Whipstitch cutout edges together; with dk. red, Whipstitch outer edges together.

4: For Bell Pull center motif, holding one unworked B to wrong side of one worked B, with dk. red, Whipstitch together. Repeat with remaining B pieces, forming Coaster.

NOTE: Cut two 9" lengths of dk. red.

5: Tie each 9" strand into a bow; glue one bow to photo frame and one to bell frame as shown in photo. For Bell Pull, trim ends of ribbon as desired or as shown; fold ribbon in half and glue photo frame, center motif frame and bell frame to ribbon as shown. ☺

COLOR KEY: Apples for Teacher

	Worsted-weight	Nylon Plus™	Need-loft®	YARN AMOUNT
■	Dk. Red	#20	#01	26 yds.
■	Black	#02	#00	15 yds.
▨	White	#01	#41	15 yds.
▧	Mint	#30	#24	1 yd.

A – Cutout Square
(cut 3) 25 x 25 holes

B – Solid Square
(cut 5) 25 x 25 holes

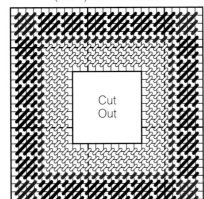

Halloween Treat Bags

Designed by Glenda Chamberlain

LEVEL OF DIFFICULTY: Average

SIZE:

Pumpkin Bag is 4½" x 6¾" x about 10" tall; Cat Bag is 4½" x 8½" x about 10" tall, including handles.

MATERIALS:

Two sheets each of orange and black and one sheet of green 7-count plastic canvas; Craft glue or glue gun; Worsted-weight or plastic canvas yarn (for amounts see individual Color Keys; Cat Bag Color Key on page 88).

Pumpkin Bag

CUTTING INSTRUCTIONS:

NOTE: Graphs continued on page 88.

A: For sides, cut four from orange 26 x 29 holes (no graph).

B: For bottom, cut one from orange 26 x 26 holes (no graph).

C: For handle and backing, cut one from black according to graph for handle and one from orange 8 x 90 holes for backing (no backing graph).

D: For pumpkins, cut two from orange according to graph.

E: For pumpkin lids, cut two from orange according to graph.

F: For pumpkin eyes and nose, cut six (four for eyes and two for nose) from black according to graph.

G: For pumpkin mouths, cut two from black according to graph.

H: For pumpkin stems, cut two from green according to graph.

STITCHING INSTRUCTIONS:

NOTE: A-C and E-H pieces are not worked.

1: Using pumpkin and Continental Stitch, work D pieces according to graph; Overcast edges of D and E pieces.

2: For bag, with orange, Whipstitch A-C pieces together according to Bag Assembly Diagram on page 88; omitting handle, Overcast edges.

D – Pumpkin Bag Pumpkin
(cut 2 from orange) 35 x 44 holes

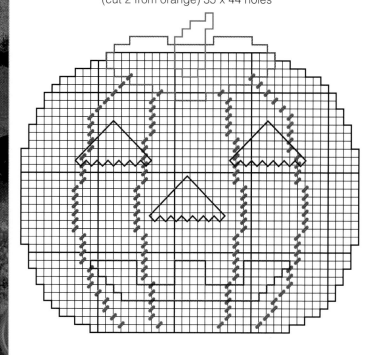

COLOR KEY: Pumpkin Bag

Worsted-weight	Nylon Plus™	Need-loft®	YARN AMOUNT
■ Pumpkin	#50	#12	22 yds.

STITCH KEY:

☐ Eyes, Nose & Mouth Placement
☐ Lid Placement
☐ Stem Placement

3: Glue one E, three F, one G and one H to each D as indicated on graph; matching bottom edges, glue D pieces to Basket sides opposite handle attachment as shown in photo.

Cat Bag

CUTTING INSTRUCTIONS:
NOTE: Graphs on page 88.
A-C: Substituting green for orange, follow steps A-C of Pumpkin Bag.
D: For cat heads, cut two from black according to graph.
E: For cat bodies, cut two from black according to graph.

F: For cat eyes, cut four from green according to graph.

STITCHING INSTRUCTIONS:
NOTE: Pieces are not worked.
1: For bag, with dk. green, Whipstitch A-C pieces together according to Bag Assembly Diagram; omitting handle, Overcast edges.

2: With gray, Overcast edges of D and E piece as indicated on graph. Glue two F pieces to each D as indicated. For cat, glue one D and one E together as shown in photo; matching bottom edges, glue one cat to each Basket side opposite handle attachment as shown. ⊕

Halloween Treat Bags

Instructions & photo on pages 86 & 87

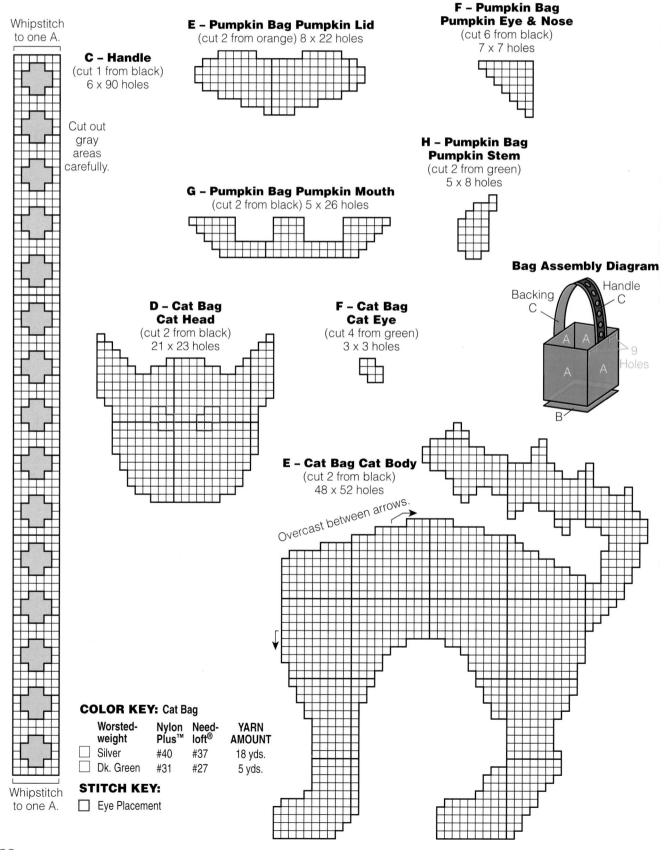

Whipstitch to one A.

C – Handle
(cut 1 from black)
6 x 90 holes

Cut out gray areas carefully.

E – Pumpkin Bag Pumpkin Lid
(cut 2 from orange) 8 x 22 holes

F – Pumpkin Bag Pumpkin Eye & Nose
(cut 6 from black)
7 x 7 holes

H – Pumpkin Bag Pumpkin Stem
(cut 2 from green)
5 x 8 holes

G – Pumpkin Bag Pumpkin Mouth
(cut 2 from black) 5 x 26 holes

Bag Assembly Diagram

Backing
C
Handle
C
A A
A A
9 Holes
B

D – Cat Bag Cat Head
(cut 2 from black)
21 x 23 holes

F – Cat Bag Cat Eye
(cut 4 from green)
3 x 3 holes

E – Cat Bag Cat Body
(cut 2 from black)
48 x 52 holes

Overcast between arrows.

COLOR KEY: Cat Bag

	Worsted-weight	Nylon Plus™	Need-loft®	YARN AMOUNT
☐	Silver	#40	#37	18 yds.
☐	Dk. Green	#31	#27	5 yds.

STITCH KEY:

☐ Eye Placement

Whipstitch to one A.

Pumpkin Patch Welcome

Designed by Kimberly A. Suber

Instructions on next page

Pumpkin Patch Welcome

Photo on page 89

LEVEL OF DIFFICULTY: Easy

SIZE:
13⅛" x 16".

MATERIALS:
2½ sheets of 7-count plastic canvas; ¼ sheet of 10-count plastic canvas; Craft glue or glue gun; Worsted-weight or plastic canvas yarn (for amounts see Color Key).

CUTTING INSTRUCTIONS:
NOTE: Use 7-count for A-C and 10-count canvas for D and E pieces.
A: For sign, cut one according to graph.
B: For large pumpkins #1-#3, cut one each according to graphs.
C: For large leaves #1 and #2, cut number indicated according to graphs.
D: For small pumpkins #1 and #2, cut one each according to graphs.
E: For small leaves, cut two according to graph.

STITCHING INSTRUCTIONS:
1: Using colors and stitches indicated, work A-C pieces according to graphs; with orange for sign and with matching colors, Overcast edges.

2: Using colors and embroidery stitches indicated, embroider facial detail on B pieces and leaf veins on C pieces as indicated on graphs.

NOTE: Separate remaining yarn into 2-ply or nylon plastic canvas yarn into 1-ply strands.

3: Using 2-ply (or 1-ply) colors and stitches indicated, work D and E pieces according to graphs; with matching colors, Overcast edges. Using forest and Straight Stitch, embroider leaf veins on E pieces as indicated.

4: Glue sign and large pumpkins together and large leaves to large pumpkins as shown in photo; glue small pumpkins to sign and small leaves to small pumpkins as shown. Hang as desired.

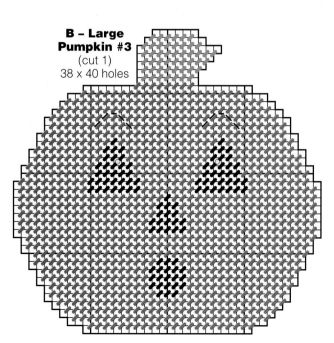

B – Large Pumpkin #3
(cut 1)
38 x 40 holes

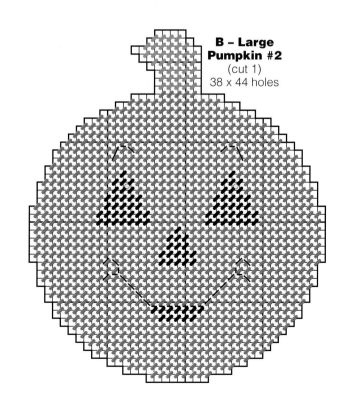

B – Large Pumpkin #2
(cut 1)
38 x 44 holes

COLOR KEY: Pumpkin Patch Welcome

	Worsted-weight	Nylon Plus™	Need-loft®	YARN AMOUNT
■	Orange	#17	#58	58 yds.
■	Black	#02	#00	30 yds.
■	Forest	#32	#29	5 yds.
■	Dk. Green	#31	#27	4 yds.
◨	Green	#58	#28	4 yds.
◨	White	#01	#41	2 yds.

STITCH KEY:

― Backstitch/Straight Stitch

● French Knot

C – Large Leaf #1
(cut 2)
8 x 8 holes

C – Large Leaf #2
(cut 3)
7 x 7 holes

E – Small Leaf
(cut 2 from 10-count)
5 x 5 holes

A – Sign
(cut 1) 34 x 80 holes

D – Small Pumpkin #1
(cut 1 from 10-count)
17 x 18 holes

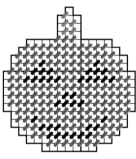

D – Small Pumpkin #2
(cut 1 from 10-count)
17 x 18 holes

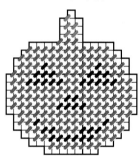

B – Large Pumpkin #1
(cut 1)
45 x 62 holes

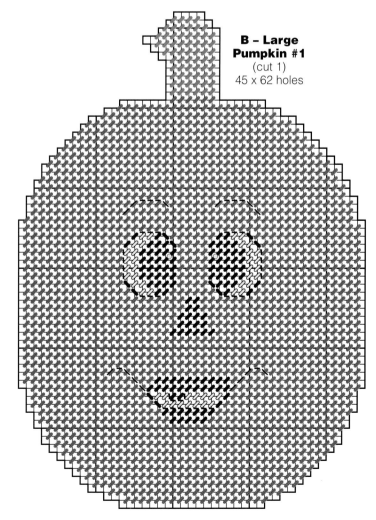

91

Spook House Tissue Cover

Designed by Nancy Dorman

LEVEL OF DIFFICULTY: Challenging

SIZE:
Snugly covers a boutique-style tissue box.

MATERIALS:
Three sheets of clear and ½ sheet of black 7-count plastic canvas; Seven small silk leaves in autumn colors; Excelsior or Spanish moss; One miniature flocked bear in Halloween costume; Polyester fiberfill (for cobwebs); Craft glue or glue gun; Six-strand embroidery floss (for amounts see Color Key on page 94); Worsted-weight or plastic canvas yarn (for amounts see Color Key.)

CUTTING INSTRUCTIONS:
NOTES: Graphs on pages 94 & 95.
Use black for J and clear canvas for remaining pieces.
A: For base, cut one according to graph.
B: For house front and back, cut one each according to graphs.
C: For house sides, cut two 31 x 35 holes.
D: For house roof pieces, cut two according to graph.
E: For chimney front and back, cut two (one for front and one for back) according to graph.
F: For chimney sides, cut two 11 x 13 holes.
G: For small shutters, cut four according to graph.
H: For large shutters, cut fourteen according to graph.
I: For porch roof, cut one 10 x 29 holes.
J: For porch posts, cut two according to graph.

STITCHING INSTRUCTIONS:
NOTES: J pieces are not worked.

Except for shutters, use Herringbone Whipstitch for Whipstitch and Herringbone Overcast for Overcast; use regular Overcast for shutters.
1: Using colors and stitches indicated, work A-I (work two G and seven H pieces on opposite side of canvas) pieces according to graphs. With matching colors, Overcast edges of A and G-I pieces.

NOTE: Separate camel into 2-ply or nylon plastic canvas yarn into 1-ply strands.

2: Using 2-ply (or 1-ply) camel and Straight Stitch, embroider pumpkin stems on A and B pieces as indicated on graphs. Using two strands gray floss and Straight Stitch, embroider cobwebs on A and B pieces as indicated. Using six strands black floss, Backstitch, Straight Stitch and French Knot, embroider ghost and pumpkin facial features on A and B pieces as indicated.

3: For house, with silver, Whipstitch B and C pieces together as indicated; Overcast unfinished edges. For house roof, holding D pieces wrong sides together, with gray, Whipstitch together as indicated; Overcast unfinished edges. For chimney, with silver, Whipstitch E and F pieces together according to Chimney Assembly Diagram on page 95; Overcast unfinished edges.

4: Glue house to cutout edges of base, house roof to house and chimney to cutout edges of roof as shown in photo. Glue porch roof and porch posts together and to house front as indicated (see photo). Glue shutters to house front, back and sides as indicated (see photo). Glue excelsior or Spanish moss to base around house and leaves and miniature bear to base and roof as desired or as shown. For cobwebs, pull apart small amounts of fiberfill until loose but not separated, then place on house as desired (see photo). ☺

Spook House Tissue Cover

Instructions & photo on pages 92 & 93

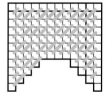

E – Chimney Front & Back
(cut 1 each)
11 x 12 holes

A – Base
(cut 1) 61 x 61 holes

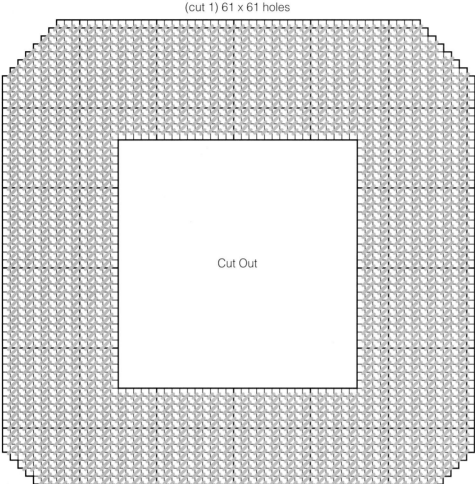

Cut Out

F – Chimney Side
(cut 2) 11 x 13 holes

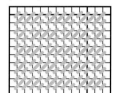

J – Porch Post
(cut 2 from black)
9 x 22 holes

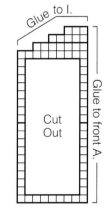

Glue to I.

Glue to front A.

Cut Out

── Whipstitch ──   **D – House Roof Piece**   ── Whipstitch ──
(cut 2)
29 x 37 holes

COLOR KEY: Spook House

Embroidery floss			AMOUNT
■ Black			3 yds.
■ Gray			2 yds.

Worsted-weight	Nylon Plus™	Need-loft®	YARN AMOUNT
Silver	#40	#37	60 yds.
Gray	#23	#38	35 yds.
Black	#02	#00	10 yds.
Orange	#17	#58	4 yds.
White	#01	#41	2 yds.
Camel	#34	#43	1/4 yd.

STITCH KEY:

☐ Shutter Placement
☐ Porch Roof Placement
☐ Porch Post Placment

B – House Back
(cut 1)
31 x 50 holes

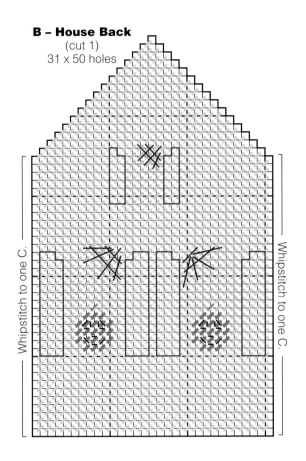

B – House Front
(cut 1)
31 x 50 holes

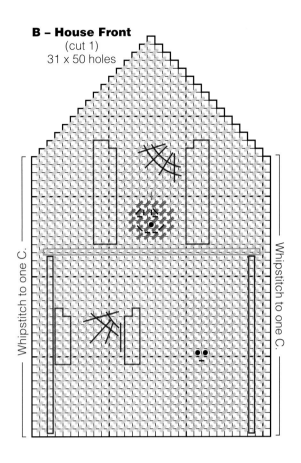

I – Porch Roof
(cut 1) 10 x 29 holes

Glue to front A.

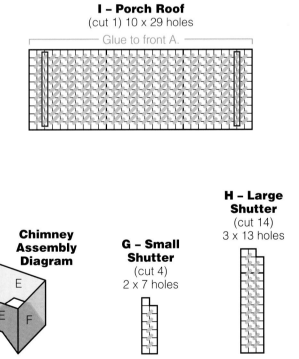

C – House Side
(cut 2) 31 x 35 holes

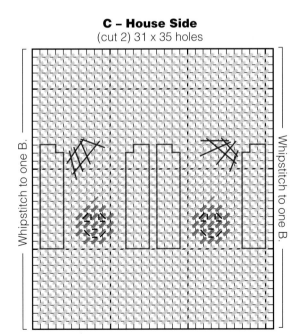

Chimney Assembly Diagram

F E
E F

G – Small Shutter
(cut 4)
2 x 7 holes

H – Large Shutter
(cut 14)
3 x 13 holes

Tricksters Welcome

Designed by Robin Will

LEVEL OF DIFFICULTY: Easy

SIZE:
16½" x 17".

MATERIALS:
Five sheets of 7-count plastic canvas; Eight purple 6-mm round acrylic faceted stones; Two 12-mm oval and two 6-mm round wiggle eyes; Two yellow ½" and one red ¼" pom-pom; Small amount blonde curly doll hair; 47 pearl 6-mm beads; Beading needle and white thread; Craft glue or glue gun; Metallic cord (for amount see Color Key on page 99); Worsted-weight or plastic canvas yarn (for amounts see Color Key).

CUTTING INSTRUCTIONS:
NOTE: Graphs on pages 98 & 99.
A: For ghost front and backing, cut two (one for front and one for backing) according to graph.
B: For pumpkin front and backing, cut two (one for front and one for backing) according to graph.
C: For spider front and backing, cut two (one for front and one for backing) according to graph.
D: For banner center front and backing, cut two (one for front and one for backing) according to graph.
E: For banner tails, cut two according to graph.
F: For mask, cut one according to graph.
G: For purse, cut one according to graph.
H: For eye patch, cut one according to graph.
I: For party hat, cut one according to graph.
J: For bow tie, cut one according to graph.

STITCHING INSTRUCTIONS:
NOTE: One of each A-D pieces are not worked for backings.

1: Using colors and stitches indicated, work one of each A-C pieces for fronts and F-J pieces according to graphs; fill in uncoded area of front C using black and Continental Stitch. Using lime and Continental Stitch, work one D for front and E pieces (work over cut corner edges).

2: With green for hat, black for banner tails and with matching colors as shown in photo, Overcast edges of E-J pieces. Using colors indicated and Straight Stitch, embroider mouths on A and C pieces as indicated on graphs.

3: For necklace, using beading needle and thread, string 12 pearls onto thread; thread ends of strand from front to back through ▲ holes on front A as indicated and secure ends at back. Sew remaining pearls to front A as indicated.

4: Holding backing A to wrong side of front A, with white, Whipstitch together. With matching colors, Whipstitch remaining front and backing B-D pieces together.

NOTE: Cut two 18" lengths of black.

5: For pumpkin eye patch, thread one end of one cut black strand through one ♥ hole on H as indicated; pull ends to even and tie into a knot. Repeat with remaining cut strand through opposite ♥ hole. Glue eye patch to front of pumpkin as shown, then twist each tie, wrap around pumpkin and glue ends to wrong side.

6: Glue stones to mask and purse as shown; glue mask and oval wiggle eyes to face and purse to one hand of ghost as shown. Glue curly hair, hat, bow tie, wiggle eyes, and pom-poms to spider as shown.

7: Glue ghost, pumpkin, spider and banner pieces together as shown. Hang as desired. ⊕

Tricksters Welcome

Instructions & photo on pages 96 & 97

I – Party Hat
(cut 1)
13 x 16 holes

F – Mask
(cut 1) 11 x 27 holes
Cut Out

J – Bow Tie
(cut 1) 8 x 10 holes

A – Ghost
Front & Backing
(cut 1 each)
66 x 90 holes

H – Eye Patch
(cut 1) 8 x 13 holes

G – Purse
(cut 1) 17 x 32 holes

Cut Out

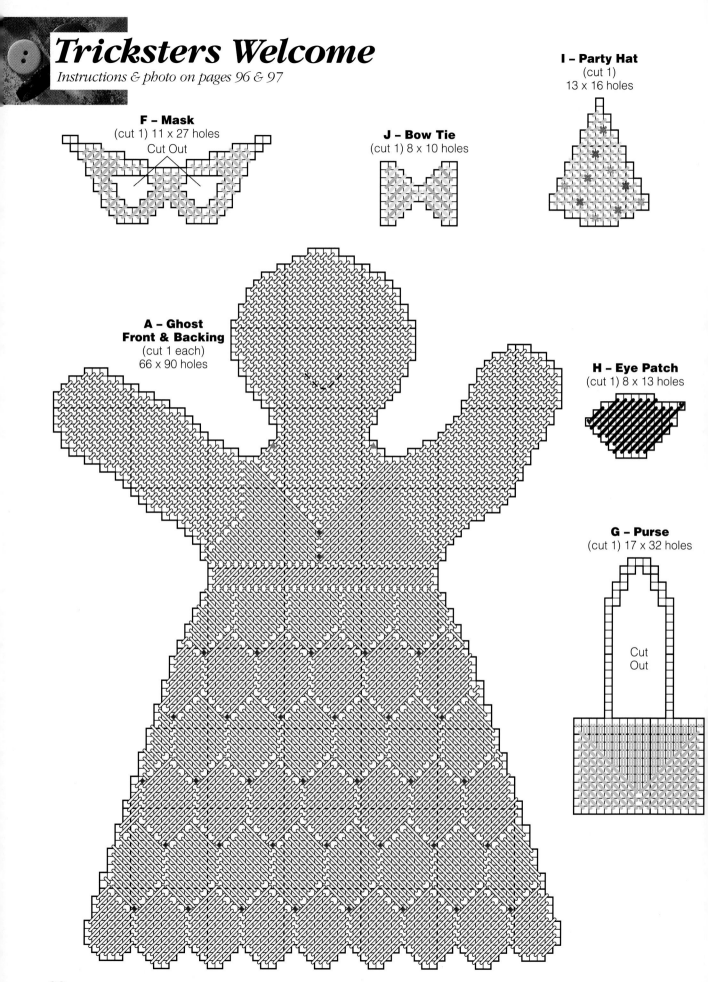

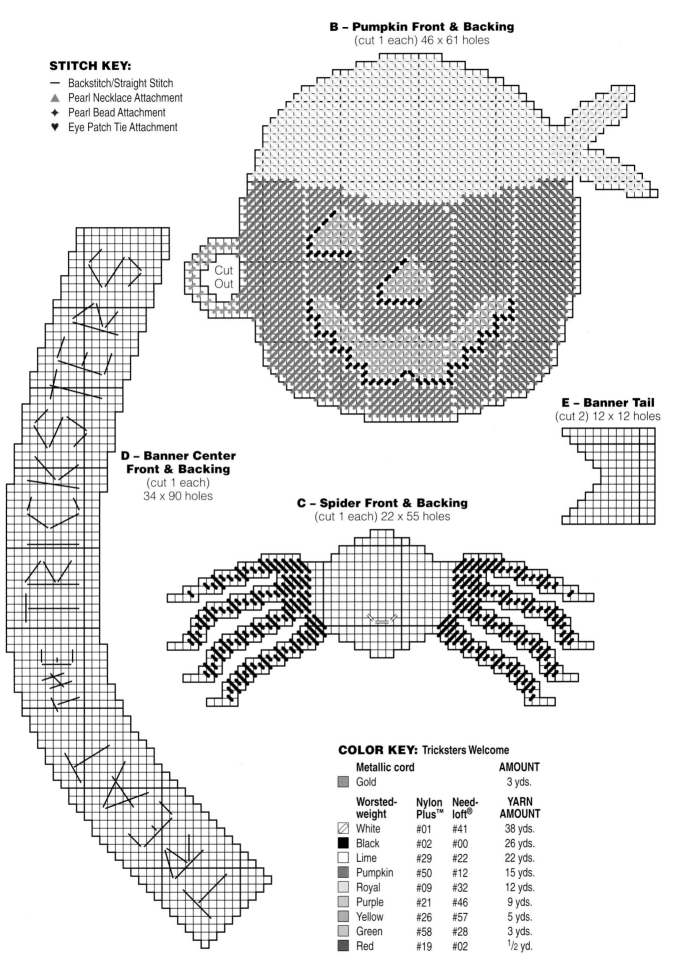

STITCH KEY:
— Backstitch/Straight Stitch
▲ Pearl Necklace Attachment
✦ Pearl Bead Attachment
♥ Eye Patch Tie Attachment

B – Pumpkin Front & Backing
(cut 1 each) 46 x 61 holes

Cut Out

E – Banner Tail
(cut 2) 12 x 12 holes

**D – Banner Center
Front & Backing**
(cut 1 each)
34 x 90 holes

C – Spider Front & Backing
(cut 1 each) 22 x 55 holes

COLOR KEY: Tricksters Welcome

	Metallic cord			AMOUNT
	Gold			3 yds.

	Worsted-weight	Nylon Plus™	Need-loft®	YARN AMOUNT
	White	#01	#41	38 yds.
	Black	#02	#00	26 yds.
	Lime	#29	#22	22 yds.
	Pumpkin	#50	#12	15 yds.
	Royal	#09	#32	12 yds.
	Purple	#21	#46	9 yds.
	Yellow	#26	#57	5 yds.
	Green	#58	#28	3 yds.
	Red	#19	#02	1/2 yd.

Mini Holiday Centerpiece

Designed by Robin Will

LEVEL OF DIFFICULTY: Average

SIZE:
Each figure is 1¾" x 2⅞" x 5" tall;
Turkey is 1¾" x 2⅞" x 2¼" tall.

MATERIALS:
1½ sheets of 7-count plastic canvas; Six black 4-mm half-round beads; Craft glue or glue gun; Worsted-weight or plastic canvas yarn (for amounts see Color Key on page 102).

CUTTING INSTRUCTIONS:
NOTE: Graphs on page 102.
A: For bases and backings, cut six (three for bases and three for backings) according to graph.
B: For girl front and back, cut one each according to graphs.
C: For boy front and back, cut one each according to graphs.
D: For turkey head and body pieces, cut two according to graph.
E: For turkey tail feathers, cut two according to graph.
F: For turkey wings, cut two according to graph.
G: For turkey feet, cut two according to graph.

STITCHING INSTRUCTIONS:
NOTE: Three A pieces for backings are not worked.
1: Using colors and stitches indicated, work three A pieces for bases and B-G (work one D on opposite side of canvas) pieces according to graphs. Fill in uncoded areas of B and C pieces using eggshell and Continental Stitch. With yellow for feet and with maple, Overcast edges of F

and G pieces.

2: Using colors and embroidery stitches indicated, embroider mouths on front B and front C and necklace chain on front C as indicated on graphs.

3: For girl dress fringe, with eggshell, work a Fringe Stitch in each ✦ hole on each B as indicated; trim ends and fray to fluff.

NOTE: Cut three 2-yd. lengths of black.

4: For girl braid, holding cut black strands together, knot together at one end. Braid strands together to 6" in length; knot together at end of braid to secure and trim away excess yarn. Holding B pieces wrong sides together with center of braid between across neck edges (see photo), with matching colors, Whipstitch together as indicated; Overcast unfinished edges of feet and legs.

5: Spread feet apart; with maple, tack feet to center of one worked A. Holding one backing A to wrong side of base, Whipstitch together.

NOTE: Cut three 1-yd. lengths of black.

6: For boy braid, holding cut strands together, knot together at one end; thread ends opposite knot from back to front through ▲ hole on back C as indicated. Pull through until knot is tight against canvas. Braid strands together to 2" in length; knot end of braid to secure and trim away excess yarn.

7: Holding C pieces wrong sides together, with matching colors, Whipstitch together as indicated; Overcast unfinished edges of feet and legs. For pant fringe, with

Continued on page 102

Mini Holiday Centerpiece

Continued from page 100

eggshell, work a Continous Lark's Head Knot through both thicknesses over each ◆ bar on C pieces as indicated; trim ends and fray to fluff. Follow Step 5.

8: For turkey head and body, holding D pieces wrong sides together, with yellow for beak, crimson for waddle as indicated and with maple (see photo), Whipstitch together. For turkey tail feath-ers, holding E pieces wrong sides together, with maple, Whipstitch together as indicated; Whipstitch unfinished bottom edges centered along fourth bar from one long edge of remaining base A. Holding remaining backing A to wrong side of base, with fern, Whipstitch together. Glue turkey pieces together and to base as shown in photo.

9: For eyes, glue beads to pieces as indicated. ☺

A – Base & Backing
(cut 3 each) 11 x 18 holes

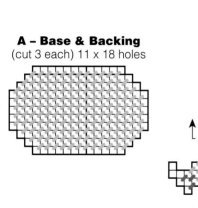

B – Girl Back
(cut 1)
26 x 26 holes

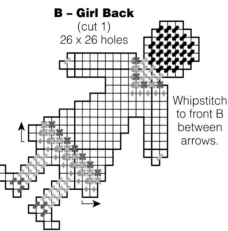

Whipstitch to front B between arrows.

B – Girl Front
(cut 1)
26 x 26 holes

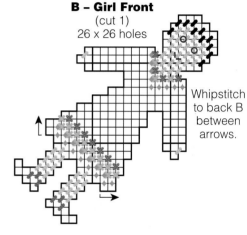

Whipstitch to back B between arrows.

D – Turkey Head & Body Piece
(cut 2)
7 x 10 holes

Glue to tail feathers.

Beak

Waddle

E – Turkey Tail Feathers
(cut 2) 13 x 19 holes

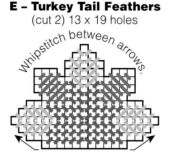

Whipstitch between arrows.

C – Boy Front
(cut 1)
26 x 26 holes

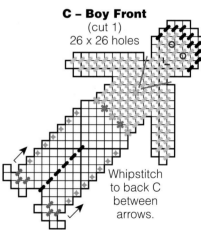

Whipstitch to back C between arrows.

COLOR KEY: Mini Holiday Centerpiece

Worsted-weight	Nylon Plus™	Need-loft®	YARN AMOUNT
☐ Eggshell	#24	#39	12 yds.
☐ Fern	#57	#23	12 yds.
☐ Maple	#35	#13	8 yds.
☐ Flesh	#14	#56	6 yds.
☐ Black	#02	#00	5 yds.
☐ Gold	#27	#17	3 yds.
☐ Rust	#51	#09	2½ yds.
☐ Yellow	#26	#57	2 yds.
☐ Turquoise	#03	#54	2 yds.
☐ Crimson	#53	#42	¼ yd.

STITCH KEY:

– Backstitch/Straight Stitch

◆ Unworked Area/Fringe Attachment

▲ Boy Braid Attachment

○ Bead Placement

F – Turkey Wing
(cut 2)
4 x 4 holes

Glue to body.

G – Turkey Foot
(cut 2)
4 x 5 holes

C – Boy Back
(cut 1)
26 x 26 holes

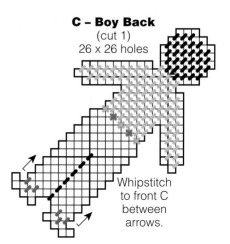

Whipstitch to front C between arrows.

Teacher's Tissues
Instructions & photo on pages 82 & 83

Bell Tower Assembly Diagram
Step 1:
Whipstitch E (hold two E pieces wrong sides together for each side) and F pieces together; Overcast unfinished edges of F pieces.

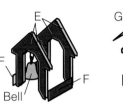

Step 3:
Whipstitch G pieces wrong sides together; Overcast unfinished edges.

Step 2:
Thread 4" strand through hole at top of bell; glue ends of strand to inside front of tower.

Step 4:
Glue roof to tower assembly.

Optional Tissue Cover
Bottom Assembly Diagram

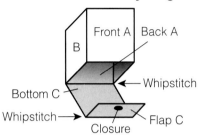

103

Christmas Cheer

As winter approaches, add the finishing touches to your handcrafted holiday decorations. When the first glow of Christmas fills the cold night air and carolers sing of the season, cozy up to the woodstove with a cup of hot cocoa and dream of Santa's surprises to come.

Santa Basket

Designed by Michele Wilcox

LEVEL OF DIFFICULTY: Easy

SIZE:
4" x 6½" x 10½" tall.

MATERIALS:
1½ sheets of 7-count plastic canvas; About 60 white, pearl and ecru ½-1" across buttons without shanks; Craft glue or glue gun; #3 pearl cotton or six-strand embroidery floss (for amounts see Color Key); Worsted-weight or plastic canvas yarn (for amounts see Color Key).

CUTTING INSTRUCTIONS:
A: For front and back, cut two (one for front and one for back) according to graph.
B: For sides, cut two 25 x 29 holes.
C: For bottom, cut one 25 x 41 holes.
D: For handle, cut one 6 x 59 holes.

STITCHING INSTRUCTIONS:
1: Using colors indicated and Continental Stitch, work pieces according to graphs; fill in uncoded areas of A using eggshell and Continental Stitch. With tangerine, Overcast edges of D.

2: Using colors indicated and French Knot, embroider eyes and nose on A pieces as indicated on graph. With white pearl cotton or six strands floss, sew buttons to each A to cover beard area as shown in photo.

3: With red, Whipstitch A-C pieces together as shown; with eggshell for hat trim and pom-pom and with red, Overcast unfinished edges.

4: Glue one end of handle to back of each pom-pom as shown. ☺

D – Handle
(cut 1)
6 x 59 holes

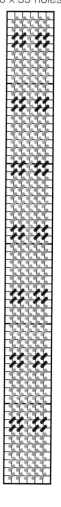

A – Front & Back
(cut 1 each)
41 x 50 holes

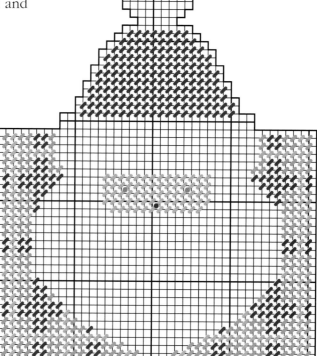

C – Bottom
(cut 1) 25 x 41 holes

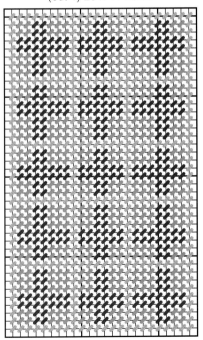

B – Side
(cut 2) 25 x 29 holes

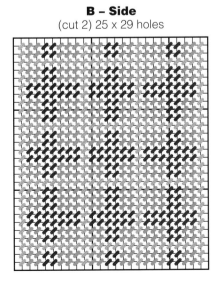

COLOR KEY: Santa Basket

#3 pearl cotton or floss			AMOUNT
☐ White			5 yds.
☐ Blue			1 yd.
■ Dk. Pink			¹/₂ yd.

Worsted-weight	Nylon Plus™	Need-loft®	YARN AMOUNT
■ Red	#19	#02	40 yds.
☐ Dk. Green	#31	#27	30 yds.
☐ Eggshell	#24	#39	25 yds.
☐ Tangerine	#15	#11	18 yds.
☐ Flesh	#14	#56	3 yds.

STITCH KEY:

● French Knot

Jeweled Snowflakes

Designed by Carolyn Christmas

LEVEL OF DIFFICULTY: Average

SIZE:
Each Snowflake is 5½" across, not including hanger; Wreath is 8" across, not including snowflake or streamers; Candy Box is 5⅞" x 2¼" tall.

MATERIALS:
Six 5" Uniek® Crafts white plastic canvas hexagon shapes; Two 6" plastic canvas radial circles; ¼ sheet (lengthwise) of 13½" x 22½" 7-count plastic canvas; 2½ yds. red 2" foil ribbon; ¼ yd. silver 1½" metallic lace ribbon or desired backing for Box lid cutout; 5 yds. white ⅛" satin ribbon; 68 clear 9-mm round faceted acrylic stones; 8" straw or styrofoam wreath; Craft glue or glue gun; ⅛" metallic ribbon or metallic cord (for amount see Color Key on page 110); Worsted-weight or plastic canvas yarn (for amount see Color Key).

CUTTING INSTRUCTIONS:
NOTE: Graphs on page 110.
A: For lid top, cut one 6" circle according to graph.
B: For lid side, cut one 6 x 125 holes (no graph).
C: For box side, cut one 14 x 121 holes (no graph).
D: For box bottom, cut away one outer row of holes from remaining 6" circle (no graph).
E: For Snowflakes #1, #2 and #3, cut two each from white hexagon shapes according to graphs. (**NOTE:** Cut off hanger loops.)

STITCHING INSTRUCTIONS:
NOTE: D piece is not worked.
1: Leaving uncoded area unworked, using dk. red and stitches indicated, work A and C (overlap holes at ends of C as indicated and work through both thicknesses at overlap area to join) according to graph and Box Side Stitch Pattern Guide. Overlapping ends four holes and working through both thicknesses

at overlap area to join, using dk. red and Slanted Gobelin Stitch over narrow width, work B. Using cord and stitches indicated, work E pieces. (**NOTE:** E pieces are not Overcast.)

2: With dk. red, Whipstitch A and B pieces together, forming lid; Overcast unfinished edges. Whipstitch C and D pieces together, forming box; do not Overcast unfinished edges.

3: Glue stones to E pieces as indicated on graph. Glue one snowflake to lid top; tie a strand of ⅛" silver metallic ribbon or cord into a bow around box lid; glue to secure (see photo). Glue wide silver lace ribbon or backing of choice to wrong side of cutout on lid top.

NOTE: For streamers, cut one 18" length of ⅛" silver metallic ribbon or cord; cut white ribbon into five uneven lengths.

4: Wrap wreath with red foil ribbon to cover, then wrap with ⅛" silver metallic ribbon or cord (see photo); glue ends to secure. Holding streamers together (fold 18" silver ribbon in half), glue ends to center of one snowflake on wrong side of canvas. Place opposite end of each streamer between two stones and glue together to secure. Glue snowflake assembly to wreath as shown.

NOTE: Cut four 12" lengths of white and four 9" lengths of ⅛" silver metallic ribbon or cord.

5: For each hanger on remaining snowflakes, thread one end of one 12" ribbon through top two holes of one snowflake point (see photo). Pull strands to even; knot ends together. Tie one 9" ribbon into a bow around hanger close to snowflake (see photo).

Box Side Stitch Pattern Guide

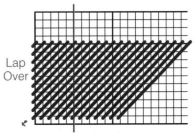

Lap Over

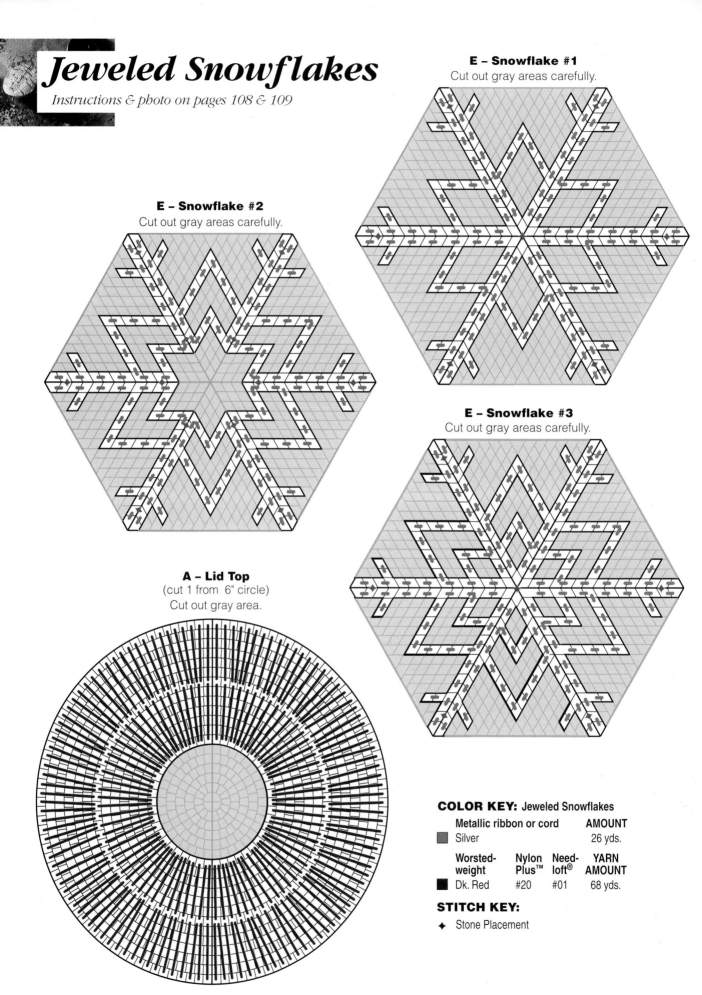

Jeweled Snowflakes

Instructions & photo on pages 108 & 109

E – Snowflake #1
Cut out gray areas carefully.

E – Snowflake #2
Cut out gray areas carefully.

E – Snowflake #3
Cut out gray areas carefully.

A – Lid Top
(cut 1 from 6" circle)
Cut out gray area.

COLOR KEY: Jeweled Snowflakes

	Metallic ribbon or cord			AMOUNT
▦	Silver			26 yds.

	Worsted-weight	Nylon Plus™	Need-loft®	YARN AMOUNT
■	Dk. Red	#20	#01	68 yds.

STITCH KEY:
◆ Stone Placement

CHRISTMAS CHEER

Cozy Snowman

Designed by Michele Wilcox

LEVEL OF DIFFICULTY: Easy

SIZE:
Snugly covers a boutique-style tissue box.

MATERIALS:
1½ sheets of 7-count plastic canvas; Four blue ¾" tinsel pom-poms; Craft glue or glue gun; #3 pearl cotton or six-strand embroidery floss (for amounts see Color Key on page 127); Raffia straw (for amount see Color Key); Metallic cord (for amount see Color Key); Worsted-weight or plastic canvas yarn (for amounts see Color Key).

CUTTING INSTRUCTIONS:
NOTE: Graphs on page 127.
A: For top, cut one according to graph.
B: For sides, cut four 30 x 36 holes.

STITCHING INSTRUCTIONS:
1: Using colors and stitches indicated, work B pieces according to graph; fill in uncoded areas and work A using lt. blue and Continental Stitch. With lt. blue, Overcast cutout edges of A.

2: Using pearl cotton or six strands floss and yarn colors indicated, Backstitch, Straight Stitch and French Knot, embroider detail as indicated on B graph.

3: With lt. blue, Whipstitch pieces together; with white, Overcast unfinished edges.

4: Glue one pom-pom to each side as shown in photo. ⊡

111

Hang a reversible garland across your mantel or along a decorated table edge.

CHRISTMAS CHEER

Cookie Chain

Designed by Carol Nartowicz

LEVEL OF DIFFICULTY: Average

SIZE:
4¼" x 35".

MATERIALS:
2 sheets of 7-count plastic canvas; Scrap of 14-count plastic canvas; 44" red ⅛" satin ribbon; Craft glue or glue gun; Six-strand embroidery floss (for amounts see Color Key); Metallic cord (for amount see Color Key); Worsted-weight or plastic canvas yarn (for amounts see Color Key).

CUTTING INSTRUCTIONS:
NOTE: Diagrams and graphs continued on page 115.

A: For Santa and gingerbread man cookies, cut three each according to graphs.

B: For round cookies, cut three each according to graphs.

C: For hearts, cut three from 14-count according to graph.

STITCHING INSTRUCTIONS:
1: Using six strands floss and yarns in colors and stitches indicated, work pieces according to graphs. Using matching colors as shown in photo, Overcast edges.

NOTE: Cut three 10" lengths of cord.

2: Wrap one 10" cord around each Santa A as shown; glue ends on back to secure. Using six strands floss, cord and yarn colors indicated, Straight Stitch, French Knot and Cross Stitch, embroider facial and clothing detail, outlines and tree decorations on A and tree B pieces as indicated on graphs.

3: Folding each end of ribbon to form 3½" loops for hanger (see Ribbon Folding Diagram on page 115), with ribbon between and spacing motifs evenly, with wrong sides together, glue each Santa A to one gingerbread A and each heart B to one tree B as shown. Glue one C to each gingerbread man as shown. ⊕

C – Heart
(cut 3 from 14-count)
8 x 9 holes

B – Heart Cookie
(cut 3)
16 x 16 holes

B – Tree Cookie
(cut 3)
16 x 16 holes

COLOR KEY: Cookie Chain

Embroidery floss			AMOUNT
Red			3 yds.
White			3 yds.
Black			1 yd.

Metallic cord			AMOUNT
Gold			2 yds.

Worsted-weight	Nylon Plus™	Need-loft®	YARN AMOUNT
Cinnamon	#44	#14	18 yds.
White	#01	#41	16 yds.
Red	#19	#02	13 yds.
Black	#02	#00	7 yds.
Dk. Green	#31	#27	4 yds.
Pink	#11	#07	1 yd.

STITCH KEY:
— Backstitch/Straight Stitch
• French Knot
✕ Cross Stitch

CHRISTMAS CHEER

Red Star Bowl

Designed by Carole Rodgers

LEVEL OF DIFFICULTY: Average

SIZE:
7" x 7" x 4¼" tall.

MATERIALS:
Five 5" plastic canvas hexagon shapes; Scrap of 7-count plastic canvas; Metallic cord (for amount see Color Key); Worsted-weight or plastic canvas yarn (for amounts see Color Key).

CUTTING INSTRUCTIONS:
A: For large sides, use four hexagon shapes.
B: For small sides, cut between bars to make four triangles from one hexagon shape. (Two triangles will not be used.)
C: For bottom, cut one 18 x 18 holes (no graph).

STITCHING INSTRUCTIONS:
NOTE: C piece is not worked.
1: Using colors and stitches indicated, work A and B pieces according to graphs.

2: With forest, Whipstitch pieces together according to Bowl Assembly Diagram; Overcast unfinished edges. ⊕

114

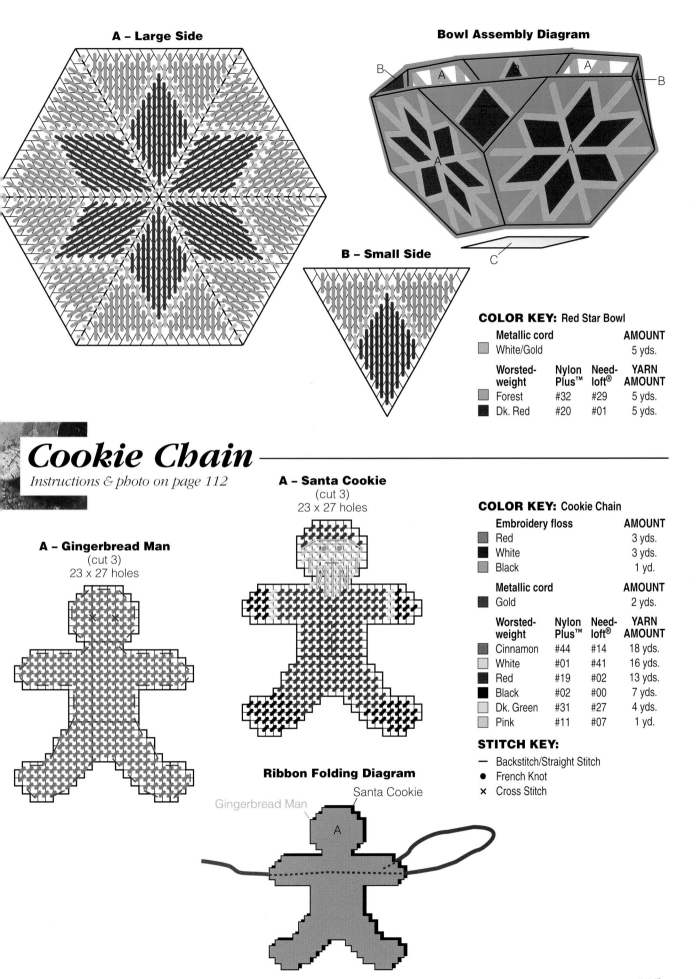

A – Large Side

Bowl Assembly Diagram

B – Small Side

Cookie Chain

Instructions & photo on page 112

A – Santa Cookie
(cut 3)
23 x 27 holes

A – Gingerbread Man
(cut 3)
23 x 27 holes

Ribbon Folding Diagram

Gingerbread Man

Santa Cookie

A

Bell & Holly

Designed by Patricia Hall

LEVEL OF DIFFICULTY:
Easy

SIZE:
13½" x 15".

MATERIALS:
Two sheets of clear 7-count plastic canvas; ½ sheet of green 7-count plastic canvas; Six red 35-mm jingle bells; Craft glue or glue gun; Worsted-weight or plastic canvas yarn (for amounts see Color Key).

CUTTING INSTRUCTIONS:

A: For Bell front and backing, cut two from clear (one for front and one for backing) according to graph.
B: For holly leaves, cut six from green according to graph.

STITCHING INSTRUCTIONS:

NOTE: Backing A piece is not worked.
1: Using colors and stitches indicated, work one A for front and B pieces according to graphs; with dk. green, Overcast edges of B pieces.

2: Holding backing A to wrong side of worked piece, with matching colors, Whipstitch together.

3: With green, tack one jingle bell to each holly leaf as indicated on B graph. Glue leaves to Bell as shown in photo or as desired. ☺

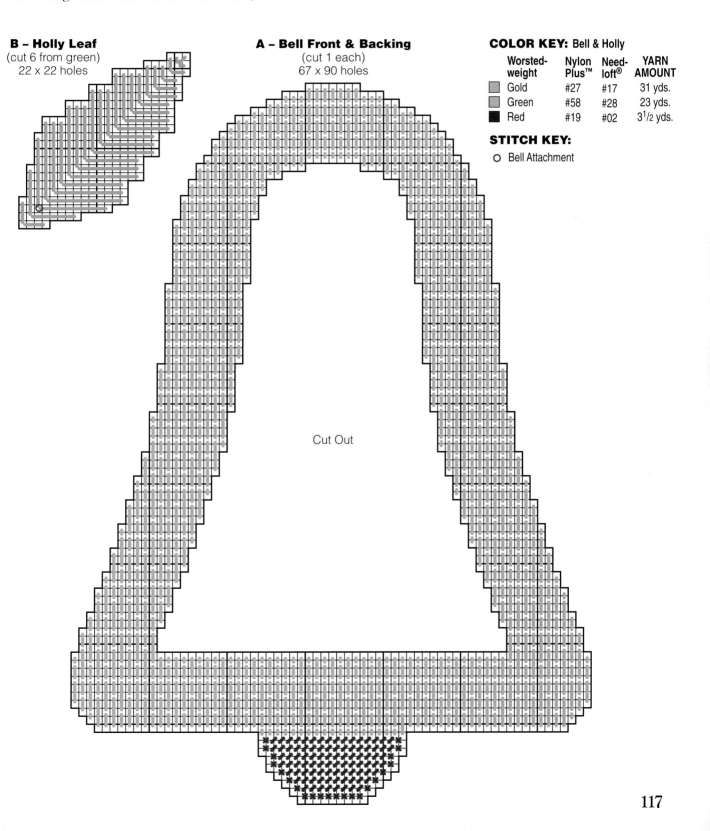

B – Holly Leaf
(cut 6 from green)
22 x 22 holes

A – Bell Front & Backing
(cut 1 each)
67 x 90 holes

Cut Out

COLOR KEY: Bell & Holly

	Worsted-weight	Nylon Plus™	Need-loft®	YARN AMOUNT
	Gold	#27	#17	31 yds.
	Green	#58	#28	23 yds.
	Red	#19	#02	3½ yds.

STITCH KEY:
○ Bell Attachment

Christmas Joy Tote

Designed by Sandra Miller Maxfield

LEVEL OF DIFFICULTY: Easy

SIZE:
3¼" x 8¼" x 13", including handles.

MATERIALS:
Two sheets of white 7-count plastic canvas; Worsted-weight or plastic canvas yarn (for amounts see Color Key).

CUTTING INSTRUCTIONS:
A: For front and back, cut two (one for front and one for back) 54 x 54 holes.
B: For side pieces, cut four 10 x 54 holes (no graph).
C: For bottom, cut one 20 x 54 holes (no graph).
D: For handles, cut two 5 x 70 holes (no graph).

STITCHING INSTRUCTIONS:
NOTE: Back A and B-D pieces are not worked.
1: Using colors and stitches indicated, work one A for front according to graph.

2: With white, Whipstitch ends of one handle to each A as indicated on graph. For Tote, with dk. red and dk. green and alternating colors as shown in photo, Whipstitch A-C pieces together according to Tote Assembly Diagram; Overcast unfinished edges. ⊕

COLOR KEY: Christmas Joy Tote

	Worsted-weight	Nylon Plus™	Need-loft®	YARN AMOUNT
▨	Dk. Green	#31	#27	22 yds.
■	Dk. Red	#20	#01	18 yds.
■	Bt. Purple	–	#64	4 yds.
▨	Silver	#40	#37	2 yds.
☐	White	#01	#41	1 yd.

A – Front & Back
(cut 1 each) 54 x 54 holes

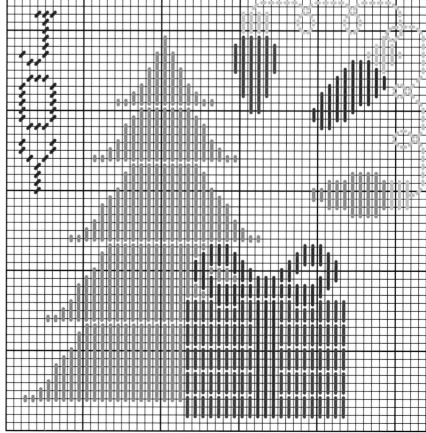

Whipstitch to D.

Whipstitch to D.

Tote Assembly Diagram

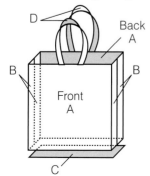

D
Back A
B
B
Front A
C

Holiday Friends

Designed by Diane T. Ray

LEVEL OF DIFFICULTY: Easy

SIZE:
Gingerman Pin is 3" x 3½"; Snowman
Pin is 3¼" x 4½".

MATERIALS:
¼ sheet of 7-count plastic canvas; Two
blue and one red 5-mm round faceted
acrylic stones; One pink 7-mm round
cabochon; Two green 7.5- x 14-mm holly
leaf acrylic stones; Four gold 6- x 9-mm
barrel pony beads; One blue sparkle and
one yellow star pony bead; One 25-mm
Santa pony bead; ⅓ yd. red metallic cord;
Two 1" pin backs; Craft glue or glue
gun; #3 pearl cotton or six-strand embroidery floss (for amount see Color Key);
Worsted-weight or plastic canvas yarn
(for amounts see Color Key).

CUTTING INSTRUCTIONS:
A: For Gingerman, cut one according to
graph.
B: For Snowman, cut one according to
graph.

B – Snowman
(cut 1)
21 x 29 holes

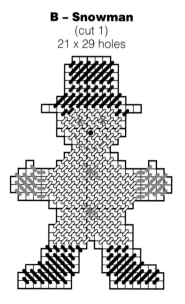

STITCHING INSTRUCTIONS:
1: Using colors and stitches indicated, work
pieces according to graphs; with matching
colors, Overcast edges.

NOTE: Separate red into 2-ply or nylon plastic canvas yarn into 1-ply strands.

2: Using 2-ply (or 1-ply) red, pearl cotton or
six strand floss and yarn colors indicated,
Backstitch, French Knot, Cross Stitch and
Smyrna Cross Stitch, embroider facial detail
and buttons as indicated on graphs.

3: Thread beads on cord as shown; tie each
end around one Snowman glove as shown
in photo and glue to secure. Glue stones to
A as shown. Glue one pin back to wrong
side of each Snowman and Gingerman.

A – Gingerman
(cut 1)
22 x 22 holes

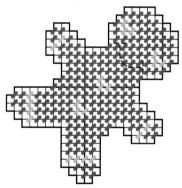

COLOR KEY: Holiday Friends

#3 pearl cotton or floss			AMOUNT
Black			1 yd.

Worsted-weight	Nylon Plus™	Need-loft®	YARN AMOUNT
Maple	#35	#13	7 yds.
White	#01	#41	4 yds.
Black	#02	#00	3 yds.
Dk. Green	#31	#27	1 yd.
Pink	#11	#07	1 yd.
Red	#19	#02	1 yd.

STITCH KEY:
— Backstitch/Straight Stitch
• French Knot
× Cross Stitch
✳ Smyrna Cross Stitch

Celestial Santa

Designed by Michele Wilcox

Instructions on next page

Celestial Santa

Photo on page 121

LEVEL OF DIFFICULTY: Easy

SIZE:
5" x 6", not including hanger.

MATERIALS:
½ sheet of 7-count plastic canvas; #3 pearl cotton or six-strand embroidery floss (for amounts see Color Key); Metallic cord (for amount see Color Key); Worsted-weight or plastic canvas yarn (for amounts see Color Key).

CUTTING INSTRUCTIONS:
A: For Side #1, cut one according to graph.
B: For Side #2, cut one according to graph.

STITCHING INSTRUCTIONS:
1: Using colors and stitches indicated, work pieces according to graphs; fill in uncoded areas using eggshell and Continental Stitch.

2: Using pearl cotton or six strands floss in colors indicated, Straight Stitch and French Knot, embroider facial detail as indicated on graphs.

3: Holding pieces wrong sides together, with matching colors, Whipstitch together.

NOTE: Cut one 12" length of cord.

4: For hanger, thread end of cord through both thicknesses as indicated, tie ends into a knot. ⊙

COLOR KEY: Celestial Santa

#3 pearl cotton or floss			AMOUNT
■ Rose			1 yd.
▨ Blue			1 yd.

Metallic cord			AMOUNT
▢ Yellow/Gold			1 yd.

Worsted-weight	Nylon Plus™	Need-loft®	YARN AMOUNT
▢ Eggshell	#24	#39	22 yds.
■ Red	#19	#02	6 yds.
▨ Flesh	#14	#56	2 yds.
▨ Rose	#12	#05	1 yd.

STITCH KEY:
— Backstitch/Straight Stitch
● French Knot
✦ Hanger Attachment

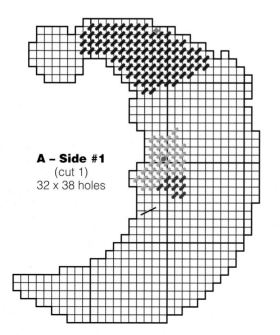

A – Side #1
(cut 1)
32 x 38 holes

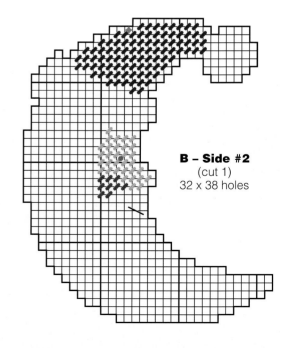

B – Side #2
(cut 1)
32 x 38 holes

Door Guard

Designed by Diane T. Ray

LEVEL OF DIFFICULTY:
Average

SIZE:
9¼" x 18½".

MATERIALS:
One sheet each of green and white 12" x 18" 7-count plastic canvas; One sheet each of black and clear standard-size 7-count plastic canvas; 6" length of black cloth-covered wire; Three small red and black feathers; one red and two green 5-mm faceted round acrylic stones; One gold 1" key ring; Craft glue or glue gun; Six-strand embroidery floss (for amount see Color Key on page 125); Metallic cord (for amount see Color Key); Worsted-weight or nylon plastic canvas yarn (for amounts see Color Key).

Continued on next page

Holiday Door Guard

Continued from page 123

CUTTING INSTRUCTIONS:

NOTE: Graphs continued on pages 126 & 127.

A: For front, cut one from green according to graph.

B: For wreath, cut one from green according to graph.

C: For interior, cut one from black according to graph.

D: For roof/front trim, cut one from white according to graph.

H – Guard
(cut 1 from clear)
32 x 90 holes

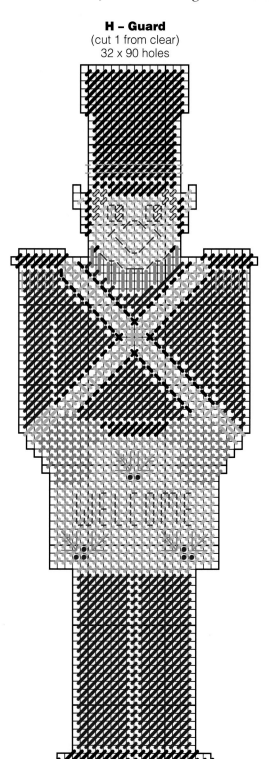

C – Interior
(cut 1 from black)
37 x 86 holes

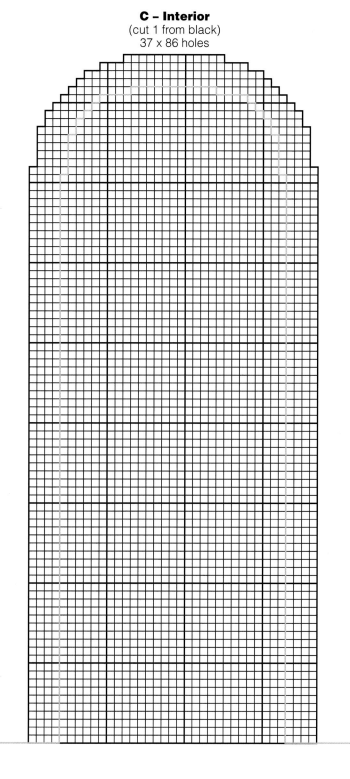

E: For door trim, cut one from white according to graph.
F: For dove body, cut one from white according to graph.
G: For dove wing, cut one from white according to graph.
H: For guard, cut one from clear according to graph.

STITCHING INSTRUCTIONS:

1: For guard house, holding D to A, E to A and A to C as indicated on graphs and working through all thicknesses as one piece, using white and stitches indicated, work pieces as indicated on graphs.

2: Using colors and stitches indicated, work B and F-H pieces according to graphs. With cord for sign and with matching colors, Overcast edges of H.

3: Using four strands floss for facial detail, six strands floss for sign and colors indicated, Backstitch/Straight Stitch and French Knot, embroider facial and uniform detail and holly on H as indicated.

NOTE: Cut one 9" length of cord.

4: Tie 9" cord into a bow; trim ends and glue to wreath as shown in photo. Glue feathers and stones to H as shown.

NOTE: Cut wire into three 3" lengths.

5: For dove's feet, bend two 3" wire pieces according to Foot Diagram. For dove eye, tie remaining wire piece into a knot. Insert ends of feet and and eye from front to back through indicated holes on F; glue to secure on wrong side. With white, Whipstitch G to right side of F as indicated.

6: With matching colors, tack wreath, dove and guard to front and key ring to back of guard house as shown. ☺

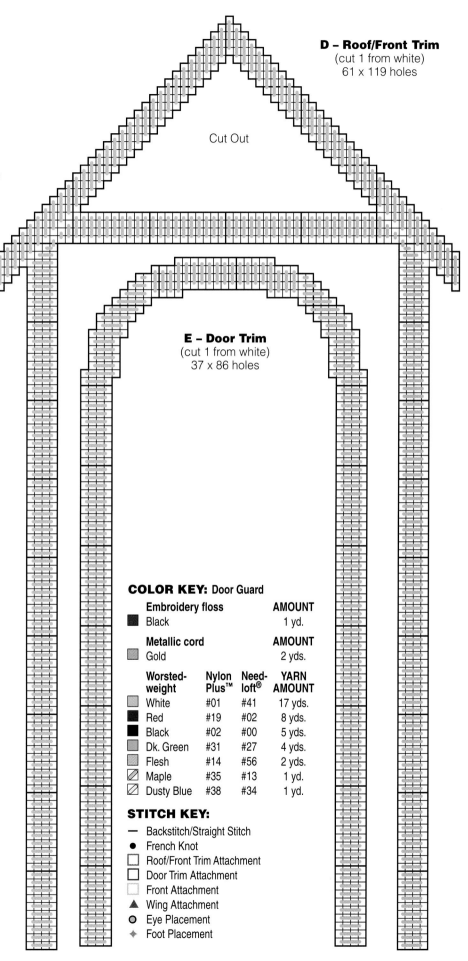

D – Roof/Front Trim
(cut 1 from white)
61 x 119 holes

Cut Out

E – Door Trim
(cut 1 from white)
37 x 86 holes

COLOR KEY: Door Guard

Embroidery floss			AMOUNT
■ Black			1 yd.
Metallic cord			**AMOUNT**
▨ Gold			2 yds.

Worsted-weight	Nylon Plus™	Need-loft®	YARN AMOUNT
▨ White	#01	#41	17 yds.
■ Red	#19	#02	8 yds.
■ Black	#02	#00	5 yds.
▨ Dk. Green	#31	#27	4 yds.
▨ Flesh	#14	#56	2 yds.
▨ Maple	#35	#13	1 yd.
▨ Dusty Blue	#38	#34	1 yd.

STITCH KEY:
- — Backstitch/Straight Stitch
- • French Knot
- ▢ Roof/Front Trim Attachment
- ▢ Door Trim Attachment
- ▢ Front Attachment
- ▲ Wing Attachment
- ◉ Eye Placement
- ✦ Foot Placement

Holiday Door Guard

Instructions & photo on page 123

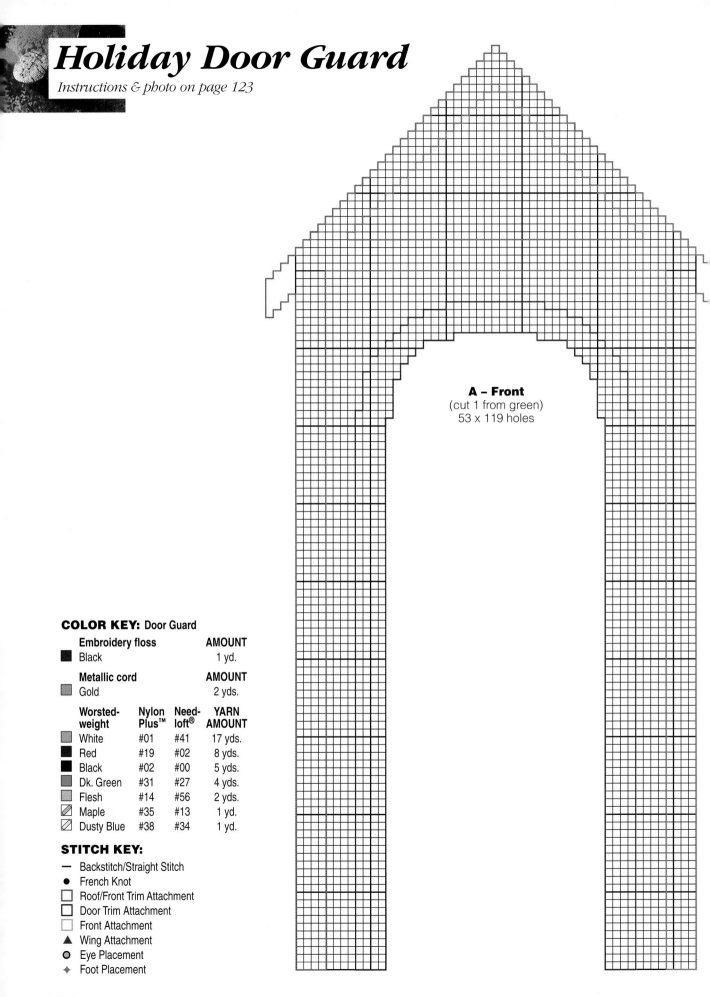

A – Front
(cut 1 from green)
53 x 119 holes

COLOR KEY: Door Guard

Embroidery floss			AMOUNT
■ Black			1 yd.

Metallic cord			AMOUNT
▨ Gold			2 yds.

Worsted-weight	Nylon Plus™	Need-loft®	YARN AMOUNT
▨ White	#01	#41	17 yds.
■ Red	#19	#02	8 yds.
■ Black	#02	#00	5 yds.
▨ Dk. Green	#31	#27	4 yds.
▨ Flesh	#14	#56	2 yds.
▨ Maple	#35	#13	1 yd.
▨ Dusty Blue	#38	#34	1 yd.

STITCH KEY:
- — Backstitch/Straight Stitch
- ● French Knot
- ☐ Roof/Front Trim Attachment
- ☐ Door Trim Attachment
- ☐ Front Attachment
- ▲ Wing Attachment
- ◎ Eye Placement
- ✦ Foot Placement

126

B – Wreath
(cut 1 from green)
20 x 20 holes

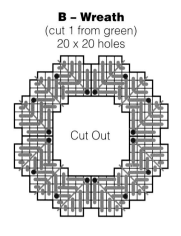

Cut Out

G – Dove Wing
(cut 1 from white)
3 x 5 holes

F – Dove Body
(cut 1 from white)
6 x 9 holes

Carefully cut away gray areas.

Foot Pattern
(actual size)

Cozy Snowman

Instructions & photo on page 111

A – Top
(cut 1) 30 x 30 holes

Cut Out

COLOR KEY: Cozy Snowman

#3 pearl cotton or floss	AMOUNT		
Blue	12 yds.		
Black	8 yds.		
Green	8 yds.		
Gold	1 yd.		

Raffia straw	AMOUNT		
Gold	4 yds.		

Metallic cord	AMOUNT		
Red/Silver	5 yds.		

Worsted-weight	Nylon Plus™	Need-loft®	YARN AMOUNT
Lt. Blue	#05	#36	45 yds.
White	#01	#41	40 yds.
Royal	#09	#32	5 yds.
Crimson	#53	#42	4 yds.
Dk. Brown	#36	#15	2 yds.
Black	#02	#00	1 yd.

STITCH KEY:

— Backstitch/Straight Stitch
● French Knot

B – Side
(cut 4) 30 x 36 holes

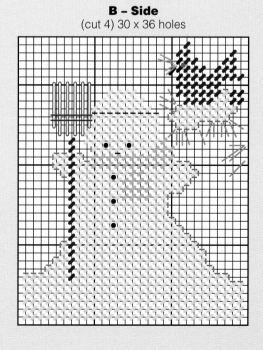

127

Fun & Games

Bring sunshine inside on rainy days with exciting playtime projects. Gather colorful skeins of yarn and canvas, and spend quality time with your youngsters as you teach them to create easy-to-make toys. Show the littlest ones how to thread buttons on yarn for a one-of-a-kind necklace.

Brighten someone's smile with a jolly clown tote bag.

Clownin' Around

Designed by Debbie Tabor

LEVEL OF DIFFICULTY: Challenging

SIZE:
4½" x 10½" x about 24" long.

MATERIALS:
Four sheets of 7-count plastic canvas; 1½" of ¾"-wide sew-on Velcro® strip; Sewing needle and white thread; ½ yd. green metallic cord; Craft glue or glue gun; Six-strand embroidery floss (for amount see Color Key on page 133); Worsted-weight or plastic canvas yarn (for amounts see Color Key).

CUTTING INSTRUCTIONS:
NOTE: Graphs and diagrams on pages 132 & 133.
A: For face, cut one according to graph.
B: For body front, cut one 36 x 36 holes.
C: For body back, cut one according to graph.
D: For pants back, cut one 12 x 36 holes (no graph).
E: For bottom, cut one 29 x 36 holes (no graph).
F: For side panel pieces #1, cut four 14 x 23 holes.
G: For side panel pieces #2, cut four according to graph.
H: For side center panels, cut two according to graph.
I: For lower arm pieces, cut two according to graph.
J: For upper arm pieces, cut four according to graph.
K: For upper leg pieces, cut four according to graph.
L: For lower leg pieces, cut four according to graph.
M: For shoe fronts and backs, cut two each according to graphs.

STITCHING INSTRUCTIONS:
1: Using colors and stitches indicated, work pieces (leave 1" Modified Turkey Work loops on A and C pieces; work two G and two J pieces on opposite side of canvas) according to graphs and stitch pattern guide. With matching colors, Overcast bottom edge of A as indicated on graph.

2: Using yarn and six strands floss in colors and embroidery stitches indicated, embroider facial detail on A and B pieces as indicated.

NOTE: Cut one 6" and one 4-yd. length of red.

3: For pom-pom, wrap 4-yd. strand around two fingers; remove wraps from fingers and tie 6" strand tightly around center of all loops. Cut through loops and trim ends to form a 1¼" pom-pom. Glue pom-pom to A as shown in photo.

4: Holding A and C pieces wrong sides together at matching upper edges, with matching colors, Whipstitch together. For hair, cut through loops; trim and fray ends to fluff.

5: For each side, Whipstitch two F, two G and one H piece together according to Side Assembly Diagram on page 132. Whipstitch B-E pieces and side assemblies together according to Tote Assembly Diagram on page 132.

6: Holding corresponding I and J pieces wrong sides together and omitting arm and leg attachment areas, with lime, Whipstitch together as indicated; with yellow, Whipstitch upper and lower arm pieces together as indicated. With lime, Whipstitch arm assembly and Tote together through all thicknesses as indicated.

7: For each upper and lower leg, holding corresponding K and L pieces wrong sides together and omitting body, leg and shoe attachment areas, with matching colors as shown, Whipstitch together. For each shoe, holding one of each M wrong sides together and omitting leg attachment area, with colors matching shoe front, Whipstitch together.

8: For each leg and shoe assembly, with dk. aqua, Whipstitch one each upper leg, lower leg and shoe together as indicated. With dk.

Continued on next page

Clownin' Around

Continued from page 131

aqua, Whipstitch leg and shoe assemblies and Tote together through all thicknesses as indicated.

NOTE: Cut metallic cord in half.

9: Tie each cord strand into a bow; glue to shoe front as shown. With thread, sew loopy side of Velcro® strip to wrong side of body back below face and fuzzy Velcro® strip to corresponding area on wrong side of body front.⊙

C – Body Back (cut 1) 36 x 39 holes

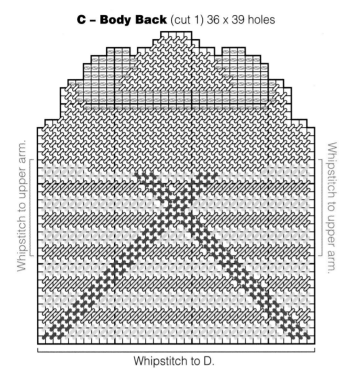

Whipstitch to upper arm.

Whipstitch to upper arm.

Whipstitch to D.

A – Face (cut 1) 16 x 36 holes

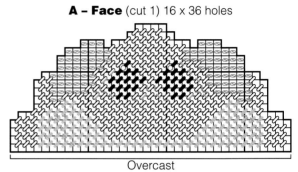

Overcast

B – Body Front (cut 1) 36 x 36 holes

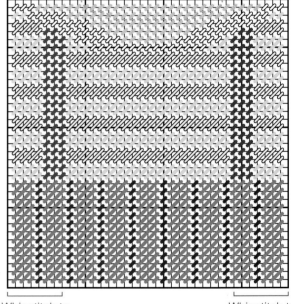

Whipstitch to upper leg.

Whipstitch to upper leg.

Side Assembly Diagram

Step 1:
For upper side assembly, with lime, Whipstitch two F pieces together.

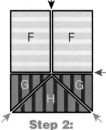

Step 3:
With dk. aqua, Whipstitch upper and lower side assemblies together.

Step 2:
For lower side assembly, with dk. aqua, Whipstitch two G and one H piece together.

Tote Assembly Diagram

Step 3:
With matching colors, Overcast unfinished edges.

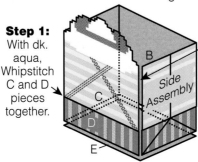

Step 1:
With dk. aqua, Whipstitch C and D pieces together.

Side Assembly

Step 2:
Omitting arm and leg attachment areas, with colors shown in photo, Whipstitch side assemblies and B-E pieces together.

F – Side Panel Piece #1
(cut 4) 14 x 23 holes

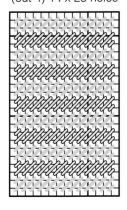

132

I – Lower Arm Piece (cut 2) 40 x 63 holes

J – Upper Arm Piece
(cut 4) 16 x 25 holes

Whipstitch to lower arm.

Whipstitch to C.

Whipstitch to upper arm.

Whipstitch to upper arm.

COLOR KEY: Clownin' Around

Embroidery floss			AMOUNT
Black			2 yds.

Worsted-weight	Nylon Plus™	Need-loft®	YARN AMOUNT
Lime	#29	#22	48 yds.
Dk. Aqua	#08	#50	47 yds.
Yellow	#26	#57	37 yds
White	#01	#41	22 yds.
Watermelon	#54	#55	20 yds.
Red	#19	#02	18 yds.
Orange	#17	#58	14 yds.
Black	#02	#00	9 yds.
Plum	#55	#59	4 yds.

STITCH KEY:
— Backstitch/Straight Stitch
● French Knot
✎ Modified Turkey Work

K – Upper Leg Piece
(cut 4) 13 x 20 holes

Whipstitch to B.

Whipstitch to lower leg.

M – Shoe Front
(cut 2) 15 x 24 holes
Whipstitch to lower leg.

M – Shoe Back
(cut 2) 15 x 24 holes
Whipstitch to lower leg.

Pants Back & Bottom Stitch Pattern Guide

Continue established pattern up and across each entire piece.

L – Lower Leg Piece
(cut 4) 20 x 21 holes

Whipstitch to upper leg.

H – Side Center Panel
(cut 2) 12 x 24 holes

G – Side Panel Piece #2
(cut 4) 13 x 14 holes

Whipstitch to shoe.

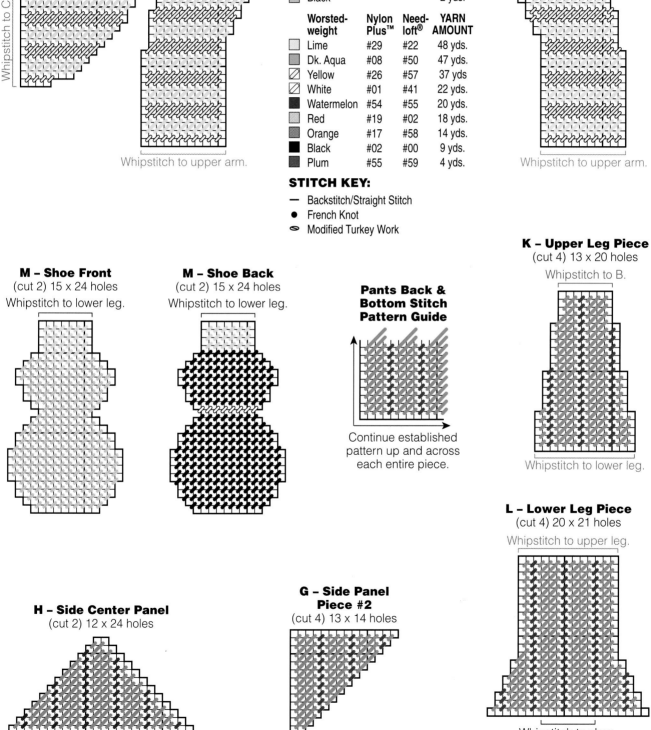

Tool Time Toys

Designed by Jocelyn Sass

LEVEL OF DIFFICULTY: Easy

SIZE:

Saw is 4½" x 8⅛"; Large Wrench is 3¼" x 7½"; Small Wrench is 2⅝" x 6½"; L Square is 5¼" x 6¼".

MATERIALS:

Two sheets of 7-count plastic canvas; ¼ yd. red ⅛" satin ribbon; Six-strand embroidery floss (for amount see Color Key); Worsted-weight or plastic canvas yarn (for amounts see Color Key).

CUTTING INSTRUCTIONS:

A: For saw, cut two according to graph.
B: For large wrench, cut two according to graph.
C: For small wrench, cut two according to graph.
D: For L square, cut two according to graph.

STITCHING INSTRUCTIONS:

1: Using colors indicated and Continental Stitch, work A and D (one of each on opposite side of canvas) pieces according to graphs; fill in uncoded areas and work B and C pieces using silver and Continental Stitch.

2: Using six strands floss and Straight Stitch, embroider inch marks on D pieces as indicated on graph.

3: For each tool, holding corresponding pieces wrong sides together, with matching colors, Whipstitch together.

4: Thread ribbon through cutouts on wrenches; tie ends into knot and trim (see photo).

COLOR KEY: Tool Time Toys

Embroidery floss			AMOUNT
■ Black			2 yds.

Worsted-weight	Nylon Plus™	Need-loft®	YARN AMOUNT
☐ Silver	#40	#37	60 yds.
Peach	#46	#47	24 yds.
Maple	#35	#13	8 yds.

STITCH KEY:
— Backstitch/Straight Stitch

A – Saw
(cut 2) 28 x 57 holes

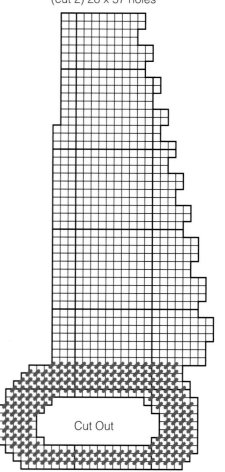

Cut Out

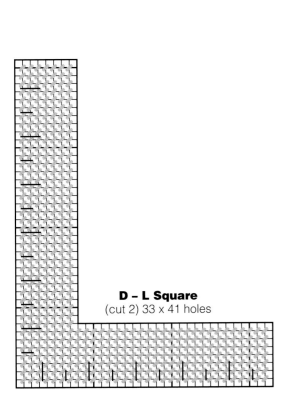

D – L Square
(cut 2) 33 x 41 holes

C – Small Wrench
(cut 2) 16 x 43 holes

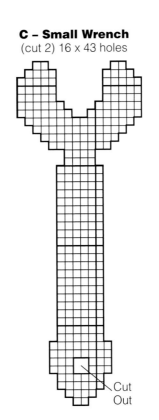

Cut
Out

B – Large Wrench
(cut 2) 20 x 49 holes

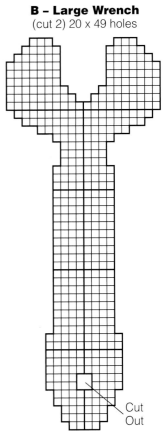

Cut
Out

'Stitches' the Cat

Artwork by Lois Sullivan

Adapted for Needlework by Sandra Miller Maxfield

LEVEL OF DIFFICULTY: Easy

SIZE:
'Stitches' doll is 8⅜" x 9¾".

MATERIALS:
2½ sheets of 7-count plastic canvas; Two green 9-mm animal eyes; ½"-wide white sew-on Velcro® strips; Sewing needle and white thread; Craft glue or glue gun; Six-strand embroidery floss (for amount see Color Key on page 138); Worsted weight or plastic canvas yarn (for amounts see Color Key).

CUTTING INSTRUCTIONS:
NOTE: Graphs on pages 138 & 139.
A: For doll, cut one according to graph.
B: For bunny suit, cut one according to graph.
C: For bunny ears, cut one according to graph.
D: For baby bunny front and back, cut two (one for front and one for back) according to graph.
E: For pilgrim dress, cut one according to graph.
F: For pilgrim hat, cut one according to graph.
G: For pilgrim turkey, cut one according to graph.
H: For Christmas dress, cut one according to graph.
I: For Christmas bow, cut one according to graph.
J: For Christmas gift, cut one according to graph.
K: For Christmas shoe #1, cut one according to graph.
L: For Christmas shoe #2, cut one according to graph.

STITCHING INSTRUCTIONS:
1: Using colors and stitches indicated, work A-C, one D for front and E-L pieces according to graphs; work remaining D for back using white and Continental Stitch. With green for Christmas bow and with matching colors as shown in photo, Overcast edges of A-C and E-L pieces.

2: Using six strands floss and yarn in colors and embroidery stitches indicated, embroider facial features on A, B (leave ½" Modified Turkey Work loops for bunny ears) and front D pieces as indicated on graphs.

3: For baby bunny, holding D pieces wrong sides together, with white, Whipstitch together.

NOTE: Cut one 12" length of dk. red; separate into 2-ply or nylon plastic canvas yarn into 1-ply strands.

4: For Christmas dress, thread ends of one 2-ply (or 1-ply) strand from back to front through ▲ holes on H as indicated; pull ends to even. Cross one end of strand over front and thread down through ♦ hole as indicated, bring straight across back and thread up through ♥ hole on opposite side; repeat two more times through remaining ♦ and ♥ holes (see photo). Reversing symbols and starting at top of dress with opposite end of same strand, thread end through ♥ and ♦ holes as for first strand end. Tie ends into a bow at front of dress as shown; tie a knot in each end to secure.

5: Cut loopy side of Velcro® into ½" and 1" pieces (**NOTE:** Fuzzy side of Velcro® will not be used.) Sew longer Velcro® pieces to backs of dresses and bunny suit and shorter Velcro® pieces to backs of remaining worked pieces, trimming Velcro® as needed to fit.

NOTE: Cut two 9" lengths of white.

6: Holding 9" white strands together, tie into a bow and trim ends as desired. Glue bow to Christmas gift and eyes to doll as shown. Velcro® strips on clothes attach to yarn on doll. ☺

Dress 'Stitches', the lovable mascot for **The Needlecraft Shop,** *in holiday finery.*

'Stitches' the Cat

Instructions & photo on pages 136 & 137

COLOR KEY: 'Stitches' the Cat

	Embroidery floss			AMOUNT
■	Black			2 yds.

	Worsted-weight	Nylon Plus™	Need-loft®	YARN AMOUNT
☐	White	#01	#41	50 yds.
☐	Tan	#33	#18	20 yds.
☐	Gray	#23	#38	15 yds.
■	Dk. Red	#20	#01	12 yds.
■	Dk. Green	#31	#27	5 yds.
■	Pink	#11	#07	5 yds.
◩	Maple	#35	#13	4 yds.
■	Black	#02	#00	2 yds.
☐	Silver	#40	#37	2 yds.
☐	Eggshell	#24	#39	1 yd.
■	Royal	#09	#32	1 yd.

STITCH KEY:

— Backstitch/Straight Stitch
● French Knot
✑ Modified Turkey Work

A – Doll (cut 1) 55 x 64 holes

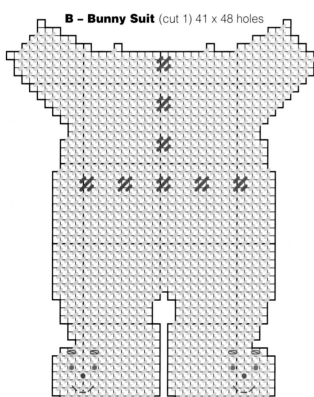

B – Bunny Suit (cut 1) 41 x 48 holes

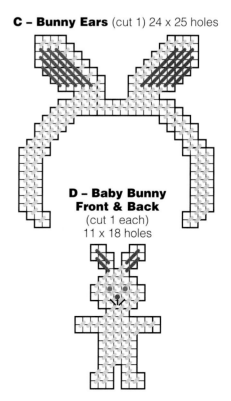

C – Bunny Ears (cut 1) 24 x 25 holes

D – Baby Bunny Front & Back
(cut 1 each)
11 x 18 holes

138

E – Pilgrim Dress
(cut 1) 45 x 50 holes

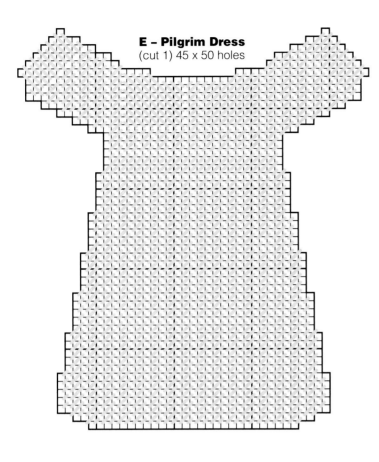

F – Pilgrim Hat
(cut 1) 18 x 27 holes

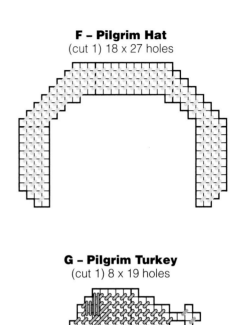

G – Pilgrim Turkey
(cut 1) 8 x 19 holes

I – Christmas Bow
(cut 1) 8 x 8 holes

J – Christmas Gift
(cut 1) 12 x 12 holes

H – Christmas Dress
(cut 1) 32 x 35 holes

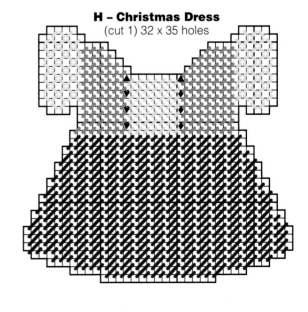

K – Christmas Shoe #1
(cut 1) 7 x 13 holes

L – Christmas Shoe #2
(cut 1) 7 x 13 holes

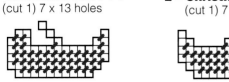

Stretch your savings when you keep extra coins in this clever bank — neck slides off body for coin retrieval.

Giraffe Coin Bank

Designed by Trudy Bath Smith

LEVEL OF DIFFICULTY: Challenging

SIZE:
5⅝" x 8" x 18½".

MATERIALS:
Three sheets of 7-count plastic canvas; Plastic lacing (for amount see Color Key on page 142); Craft glue or glue gun; Worsted weight or plastic canvas yarn (for amounts see Color Key).

CUTTING INSTRUCTIONS:
NOTE: Graphs on pages 142-144.
A: For head and neck pieces #1 and #2, cut one each according to graphs.
B: For head top slot, cut one according to graph.
C: For body sides #1 and #2, cut one each according to graphs.
D: For body front, cut one according to graph.
E: For body back, cut one according to graph.
F: For bottom, cut one according to graph.
G: For body neck piece, cut one according to graph.
H: For front legs #1 and #2, cut one each according to graphs.
I: For hind legs #1 and #2, cut one each according to graphs.
J: For ears, cut two according to graph.
K: For horns, cut two according to graph.

STITCHING INSTRUCTIONS:
NOTE: F is not worked.
1: Using colors and stitches indicated, work A-E and H-K pieces according to graphs. Fill in uncoded eye area of A#1 using white and Reverse Continental Stitch; fill in uncoded eye area of A#2 using white and Continental Stitch. With matching colors, Overcast edges of H-I, K pieces and cutout edges of B.

2: Using colors and embroidery stitches indicated, embroider facial features (**NOTE:** Use a doubled strand of maple and a doubled strand of black only for eyes) on A pieces as indicated on graphs.

3: Holding edges wrong sides together, with yellow, tightly Whipstitch cutout area of each A piece together according to Dart Illustration. With maple for mane edges (use Loop Whipstitch) and with yellow, Whipstitch A and B pieces together as indicated and according to Head & Neck Assembly Diagram; Overcast unfinished edges of A pieces.

4: Holding edges wrong sides together, with yellow, tightly Whipstitch cutout area of each C piece together according to Dart Illustration. Holding edges wrong sides together, Whipstitch X edges of each C piece together; Whipstitch C-G pieces together as indicated and according to Body Assembly Diagram; do not Overcast unfinished edges.

5: For each ear, holding edges right sides together, Whipstitch cut edges of each J piece together; with matching colors, Overcast unfinished edges.

NOTE: Cut three 18" lengths of yellow and two 3" lengths of maple.

6: For tail, holding yellow strands together, thread through ▲ holes on C pieces as indicated; pull to even. Separate strands into three equal sections; braid sections together and glue ends to secure braid. Fold maple strands in half around end of tail; glue to secure.

7: Glue ears and horns to head as indicated and legs to body sides as shown. Slide neck over neck area of body (see photo). ☺

Giraffe Coin Bank

Instructions & photo on pages 140 & 141

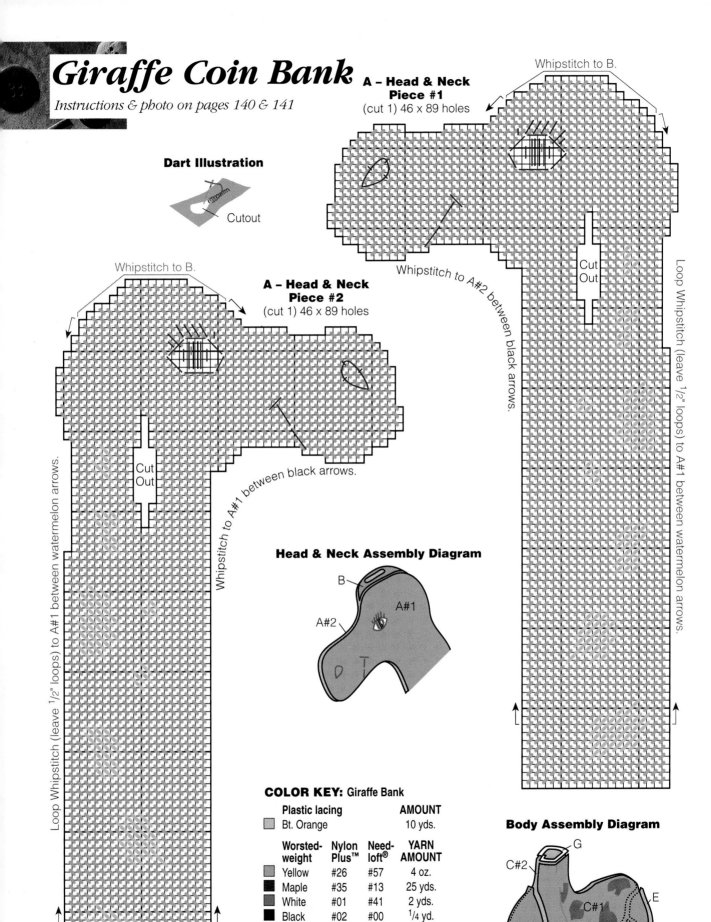

Dart Illustration

Cutout

A – Head & Neck Piece #1
(cut 1) 46 x 89 holes

Whipstitch to B.

Whipstitch to A#2 between black arrows.

Cut Out

Loop Whipstitch (leave ½" loops) to A#1 between watermelon arrows.

Whipstitch to B.

A – Head & Neck Piece #2
(cut 1) 46 x 89 holes

Cut Out

Whipstitch to A#1 between black arrows.

Loop Whipstitch (leave ½" loops) to A#1 between watermelon arrows.

Head & Neck Assembly Diagram

B
A#1
A#2

COLOR KEY: Giraffe Bank

	Plastic lacing			AMOUNT
	Bt. Orange			10 yds.

	Worsted-weight	Nylon Plus™	Need-loft®	YARN AMOUNT
	Yellow	#26	#57	4 oz.
	Maple	#35	#13	25 yds.
	White	#01	#41	2 yds.
	Black	#02	#00	¼ yd.

STITCH KEY:
— Backstitch/Straight Stitch
↤↦ Couching Stitch
▲ Tail Attachment

Body Assembly Diagram

G
C#2
C#1
D
E
F

142

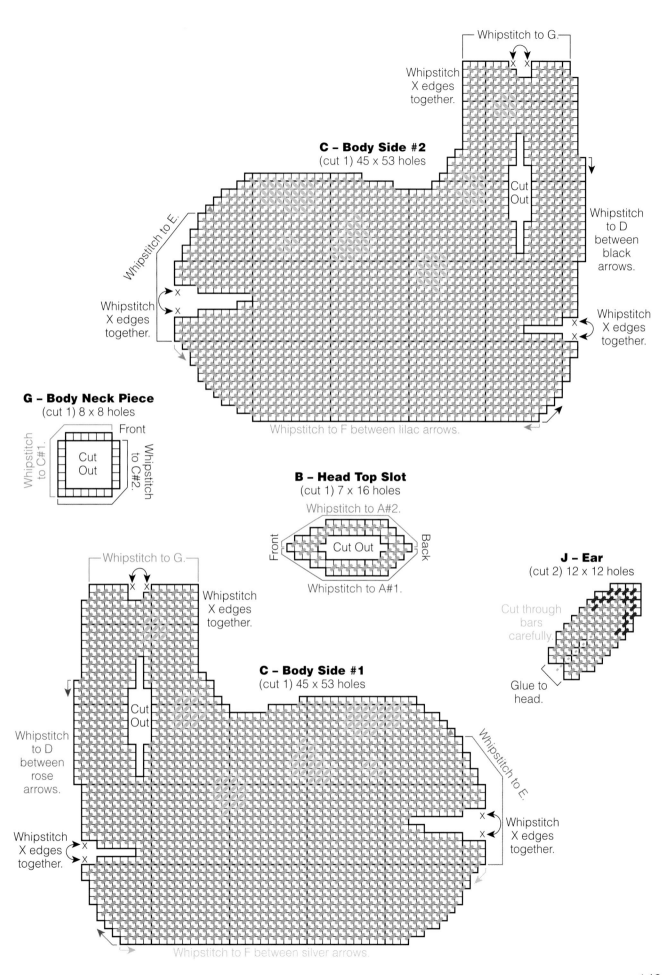

Whipstitch to G.

Whipstitch X edges together.

C – Body Side #2
(cut 1) 45 x 53 holes

Cut Out

Whipstitch to E.

Whipstitch X edges together.

Whipstitch to D between black arrows.

Whipstitch X edges together.

Whipstitch to F between lilac arrows.

G – Body Neck Piece
(cut 1) 8 x 8 holes

Front

Whipstitch to C#1.

Cut Out

Whipstitch to C#2.

B – Head Top Slot
(cut 1) 7 x 16 holes

Whipstitch to A#2.

Front

Cut Out

Back

Whipstitch to A#1.

Whipstitch to G.

Whipstitch X edges together.

C – Body Side #1
(cut 1) 45 x 53 holes

Cut Out

Whipstitch to D between rose arrows.

Whipstitch X edges together.

Whipstitch to E.

Whipstitch X edges together.

Whipstitch to F between silver arrows.

J – Ear
(cut 2) 12 x 12 holes

Cut through bars carefully.

Glue to head.

143

Giraffe Coin Bank

Instructions & photo on pages 140 & 141

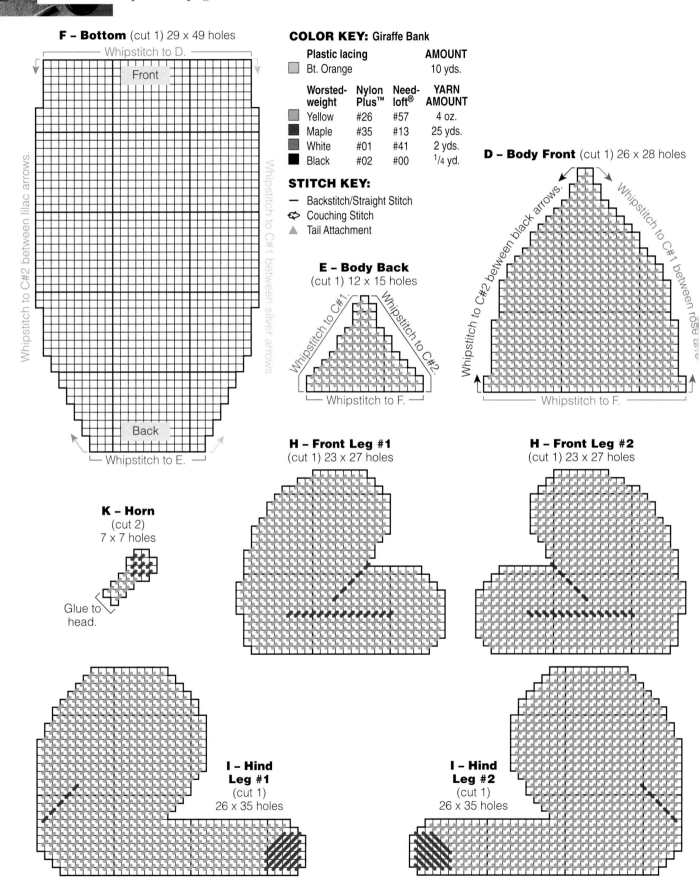

F – Bottom (cut 1) 29 x 49 holes

Whipstitch to D.

Front

Back

Whipstitch to C#2 between lilac arrows.

Whipstitch to C#1 between silver arrows.

Whipstitch to E.

COLOR KEY: Giraffe Bank

Plastic lacing			AMOUNT
Bt. Orange			10 yds.

Worsted-weight	Nylon Plus™	Need-loft®	YARN AMOUNT
Yellow	#26	#57	4 oz.
Maple	#35	#13	25 yds.
White	#01	#41	2 yds.
Black	#02	#00	1/4 yd.

STITCH KEY:
- — Backstitch/Straight Stitch
- ✧ Couching Stitch
- ▲ Tail Attachment

E – Body Back
(cut 1) 12 x 15 holes

Whipstitch to C#1.

Whipstitch to C#2.

Whipstitch to F.

D – Body Front (cut 1) 26 x 28 holes

Whipstitch to C#2 between black arrows.

Whipstitch to C#1 between rose a...

Whipstitch to F.

K – Horn
(cut 2)
7 x 7 holes

Glue to head.

H – Front Leg #1
(cut 1) 23 x 27 holes

H – Front Leg #2
(cut 1) 23 x 27 holes

I – Hind Leg #1
(cut 1)
26 x 35 holes

I – Hind Leg #2
(cut 1)
26 x 35 holes

Crayon Basket

Designed by Michele Wilcox

LEVEL OF DIFFICULTY: Easy

SIZE:
3¾" x 5⅝" x 7¼" tall, including handle.

MATERIALS:
One sheet of 7-count plastic canvas; Craft glue or glue gun; Worsted-weight or plastic canvas yarn (for amounts see Color Key on page 150).

CUTTING INSTRUCTIONS:
NOTE: Graphs on page 150.

A: For sides, cut two according to graph.
B: For ends, cut two according to graph.
C: For bottom, cut one 23 x 35 holes.
D: For handle, cut one 5 x 69 holes (no graph).

STITCHING INSTRUCTIONS:
1: Using colors and stitches indicated, work A-C pieces according to graphs. Using sail blue and Scotch Stitch over four bars, work D. With sail blue, Overcast edges of D.

2: With sail blue for bottom and with matching colors as shown in photo, Whipstitch A-C pieces together; with matching colors, Overcast unfinished edges.

3: Glue handle ends inside Basket as shown. ☺

Hoedown!

Designed by Sandra Miller Maxfield & Susie Spier Maxfield

LEVEL OF DIFFICULTY: Challenging

SIZE:
10" across x 27½" long.

MATERIALS:
Three sheets of 7-count plastic canvas; Three pairs of 7-mm wiggle eyes; Six red 4-mm faceted round acrylic beads; Three black 3-mm pom-poms; Sewing needle and white thread; One of each 15-mm, 20-mm and 25-mm gold jingle bell; 2½ yds. blue pearlized metallic cord; Craft glue or glue gun; Metallic cord (for amount see Color Key on page 148); Worsted-weight or plastic canvas yarn (for amounts see Color

CUTTING INSTRUCTIONS:
NOTE: Graphs and diagrams on pages 148 & 149.
A: For keyboard panel pieces, cut two 25 x 87 holes (no graph).
B: For keyboard black keys, cut fifteen 3 x 13 holes.
C: For keyboard inner supports, cut three 20 x 26 holes (no graph).
D: For cat bodies, cut three according to graph.
E: For cat heads, cut three according to graph.
F: For cat arms, cut six according to graph.
G: For cat legs, cut six 5 x 9 holes.
H: For cat tails, cut three according to graph.
I: For cat muzzles, cut three according to graph.
J: For cat ears, cut six according to graph.
K: For cat boots #1 and #2, cut three each according to graphs.
L: For trumpet, cut one according to graph.
M: For guitar, cut one according to graph.
N: For drum, cut one according to graph.
O: For drumsticks, cut two according to graph.
P: For mouse bodies, cut three according to graph.

Q: For mouse heads, cut three according to graph.
R: For mouse ears #1 and #2, cut three each according to graphs.
S: For mouse hands, cut six according to graph.
T: For mouse arms, cut six according to graph.
U: For mouse legs, cut six according to graph.
V: For mouse feet #1 and #2, cut three each according to graphs.

STITCHING INSTRUCTIONS:
NOTE: C pieces are not worked.
1: For keyboard panel, overlapping three holes at short ends of A pieces, using sewing needle and white thread, sew ends together through both thicknesses at each overlapped area to join. Using colors and stitches indicated and working through both thicknesses at overlap areas as one, work A pieces according to Keyboard Panel Stitch Pattern Guide and B pieces according to graph; with black, Overcast edges of keyboard panel and B pieces.

2: For gray/black cat, using colors indicated and Continental Stitch, work one of each D, E, H, I, K#1 and K#2 pieces, two F (one on opposite side of canvas), two G, two J, and L piece according to graphs. With silver for body, head, arms, legs and tail, black for ears, cinnamon for boot bottoms as indicated on K graphs and with matching colors, Overcast edges of pieces.

3: For tangerine/black cat, substituting tangerine for silver and silver for white and using colors and stitches indicated, work one of each D, E, H, I, K#1 and K#2 pieces, two F (one on opposite side of canvas), two G, two J, N and O pieces according to graphs. With black for body, head, arms, ears, tail and legs, white/gold cord for drum, cinnamon for boot bottoms as indicated and with matching colors, Overcast edges of pieces. Using white/gold and embroidery stitches indicated, embroider drum detail on N as indicated.

Continued on page 148

Kick up your heels with a trio of dancing mice and two-step to the tune of a kitty band mobile.

Hoedown!

Continued from page 146

4: For yellow cat, substituting yellow for black and silver and black for white only on boots, using colors indicated and Continental Stitch, work remaining D-K (one F on opposite side of canvas) pieces and M piece according to graphs. With yellow for ears, cinnamon for boot bottoms as indicated and with matching colors, Overcast edges of pieces. Using cinnamon and Straight Stitch, embroider guitar detail on M as indicated.

5: For mice, using colors indicated and Continental Stitch, work P-R and V pieces according to graphs. With silver, Overcast edges of P-V pieces.

6: For each cat assembly, glue corresponding pieces together according to Cat Assembly Diagrams. Glue two eyes to each cat (see photo).

NOTE: Cut three 4" lengths of silver.

7: For each mouse, glue corresponding pieces together according to Mouse Assembly Diagrams. Glue two red stones and one pompom to each head front and one 4" strand of silver to back of body for tail (see photo); tie a knot at end of each strand.

NOTE: Cut blue cord into one 24", one 18" and four 12" lengths.

8: Assemble keyboard panel, B and C pieces, cat and mice assemblies, cut cord strands and bells according to Mobile Assembly Diagram. ☺

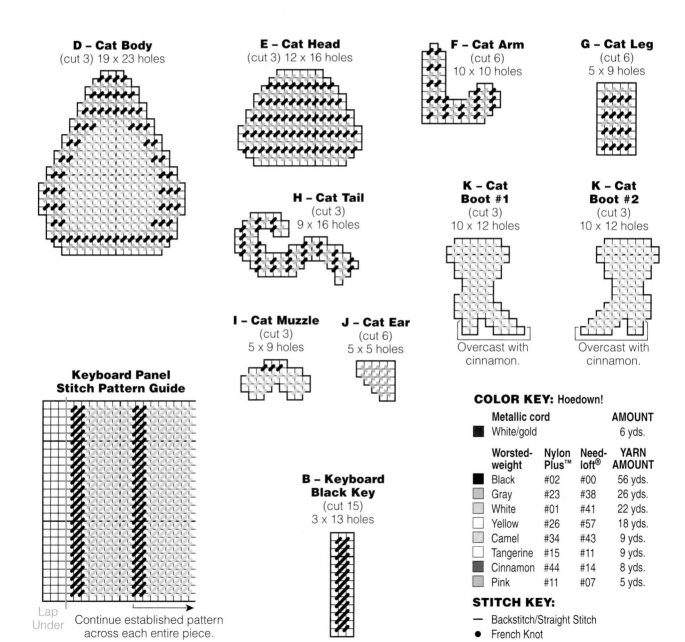

D – Cat Body
(cut 3) 19 x 23 holes

E – Cat Head
(cut 3) 12 x 16 holes

F – Cat Arm
(cut 6)
10 x 10 holes

G – Cat Leg
(cut 6)
5 x 9 holes

H – Cat Tail
(cut 3)
9 x 16 holes

K – Cat Boot #1
(cut 3)
10 x 12 holes
Overcast with cinnamon.

K – Cat Boot #2
(cut 3)
10 x 12 holes
Overcast with cinnamon.

I – Cat Muzzle
(cut 3)
5 x 9 holes

J – Cat Ear
(cut 6)
5 x 5 holes

Keyboard Panel Stitch Pattern Guide

Lap Under

Continue established pattern across each entire piece.

B – Keyboard Black Key
(cut 15)
3 x 13 holes

COLOR KEY: Hoedown!

	Metallic cord			AMOUNT
■	White/gold			6 yds.

	Worsted-weight	Nylon Plus™	Need-loft®	YARN AMOUNT
■	Black	#02	#00	56 yds.
▨	Gray	#23	#38	26 yds.
▨	White	#01	#41	22 yds.
□	Yellow	#26	#57	18 yds.
▨	Camel	#34	#43	9 yds.
□	Tangerine	#15	#11	9 yds.
▨	Cinnamon	#44	#14	8 yds.
▨	Pink	#11	#07	5 yds.

STITCH KEY:

— Backstitch/Straight Stitch

● French Knot

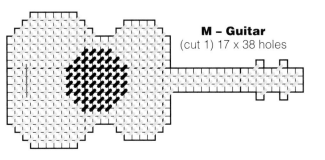

M – Guitar
(cut 1) 17 x 38 holes

O – Drumstick
(cut 2) 3 x 14 holes

N – Drum (cut 1) 16 x 21 holes

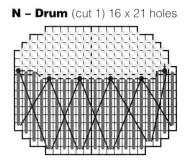

Cat Assembly Diagrams
(Instruments are shown in different colors for contrast.)

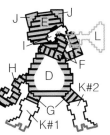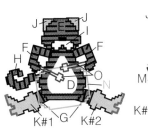

L – Trumpet
(cut 1) 12 x 19 holes

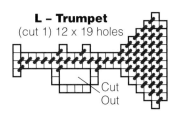

Cut
Out

Mouse Assembly Diagrams

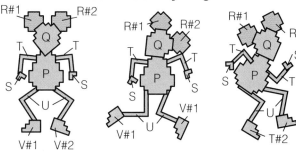

P – Mouse Body
(cut 3) 9 x 11 holes

**Q – Mouse
Head**
(cut 3)
7 x 7 holes

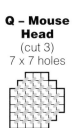

Mobile Assembly Diagram

Step 5:
Secure one end of each remaining 12" strand to top of
each support; leaving a 1" loop between knots, knot
opposite ends together twice, forming hanger.

**R – Mouse
Ear #1**
(cut 3)
5 x 5 holes

**R – Mouse
Ear #2**
(cut 3)
5 x 5 holes

Step 1:
With black,
Whipstitch C
pieces together
at one short
end; Overcast
opposite short
ends.

Yellow
Cat

12"
Strand

Keyboard
Panel

Step 2:
Glue supports
inside keyboard
panel.

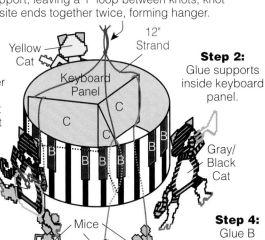

Gray/
Black
Cat

**S – Mouse
Hand**
(cut 6)
2 x 2 holes

**T – Mouse
Arm**
(cut 6)
5 x 5 holes

Tangerine/
Black Cat

Step 3:
Wrap 24", 18"
and one 12"
strand around
each support
and tie into a
knot at bottom to
secure; tie bells
to opposite
ends.

Mice

Step 4:
Glue B
pieces and
cats to
keyboard
and mice to
strands in
order shown.

**U – Mouse
Leg**
(cut 6)
8 x 8 holes

**V – Mouse
Foot #2**
(cut 3)
3 x 5 holes

**V – Mouse
Foot #1**
(cut 3)
3 x 5 holes

12"
Strand

18"
Strand

24"
Strand

15-mm
Bell

20-mm
Bell

25-mm
Bell

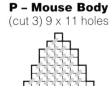

Crayon Basket

Instructions & photo on page 145

A – Side (cut 2) 25 x 35 holes

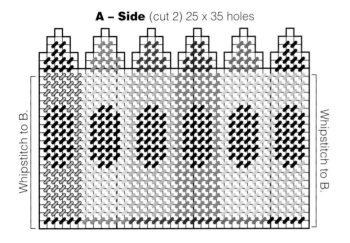

Whipstitch to B.

Whipstitch to B.

C – Bottom (cut 1) 23 x 35 holes

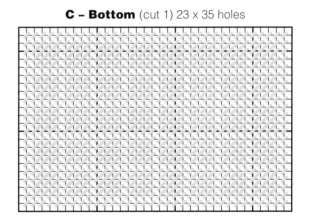

B – End (cut 2) 23 x 25 holes

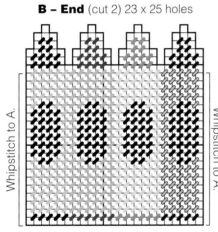

Whipstitch to A.

Whipstitch to A.

COLOR KEY: Crayon Basket

	Worsted-weight	Nylon Plus™	Need-loft®	YARN AMOUNT
	Sail Blue	#04	#35	25 yds.
	Black	#02	#00	13 yds.
	Gray	#23	#38	9 yds.
	Lt. Green	#28	#26	9 yds.
	Pink	#11	#07	9 yds.
	Tangerine	#15	#11	9 yds.
	Lavender	#22	#45	5 yds.
	Watermelon	#54	#55	4 yds.
	Dk. Green	#31	#27	4 yds.
	Dk. Orange	#18	#52	4 yds.
	Purple	#21	#46	3 yds.
	Royal	#09	#32	3 yds.

150

Little Miss Mirror

Designed by Michele Wilcox

*Instructions
on next page*

Little Miss Mirror

Photo on page 151

LEVEL OF DIFFICULTY: Average

SIZE:

8¼" x 13", not including hair.

MATERIALS:

One sheet of 7-count plastic canvas; 3" x 4" oval mirror; ½ yd. white ¼" satin ribbon; ¼ yd. white ½" ruffled lace; Craft glue or glue gun; #3 pearl cotton or six-strand embroidery floss (for amount see Color Key); Worsted-weight or plastic canvas yarn (for amounts see Color Key).

CUTTING INSTRUCTIONS:

A: For upper body, cut one according to graph.
B: For lower body, cut one according to graph.
C: For arm #1, cut one according to graph.
D: For arm #2, cut one according to graph.

STITCHING INSTRUCTIONS:

1: Using colors and stitches indicated, work pieces according to graphs; fill in uncoded areas of A and B pieces using white and Continental Stitch. With matching colors as shown in photo, Overcast edges of pieces.

2: Using pearl cotton or six strands floss and French Knot, embroider eye detail on A as indicated on graph.

NOTE: Cut thirty-six ⅔-yd. and five 6" lengths of lemon.

3: For hair, assemble cut strands according to Hair Assembly Diagram.

NOTE: Cut lace and ribbon in half.

4: For sock trim, with ends at back, wrap one lace piece around each leg as shown; glue to secure. Glue upper body to back of lower body and arms and mirror to front of assembly as shown. Tie one ribbon into a bow around end of each braid as shown; trim ends as desired. ⊡

Hair Assembly Diagram

Step 1:
Tie one short strand into a knot around center of all long strands, forming part; glue to top of head.

Step 3:
For each braid, divide long strands below second knot into three equal sections and braid together 3½" long; tie one small strand into a knot around end of braid to secure.

Step 2:
Tie one small strand into a knot around long strands 2" from each side of part; glue to head.

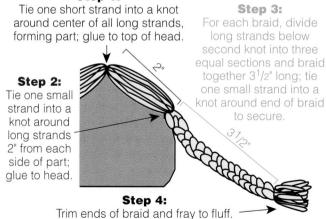

Step 4:
Trim ends of braid and fray to fluff.

COLOR KEY: Little Miss Mirror

#3 pearl cotton or floss			AMOUNT
White			¼ yd.

Worsted-weight	Nylon Plus™	Need-loft®	YARN AMOUNT
▨ Lemon	#25	#20	25 yds.
■ Watermelon	#54	#55	18 yds.
□ White	#01	#41	18 yds.
▦ Flesh	#14	#56	12 yds.
▤ Lt. Green	#28	#26	10 yds
▨ Navy	#45	#31	5 yds.
▥ Sail Blue	#04	#35	2 yds.

STITCH KEY:

● French Knot

A – Upper Body (cut 1) 35 x 47 holes

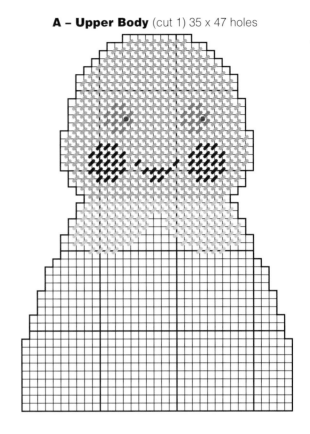

C – Arm #1
(cut 1)
16 x 28 holes

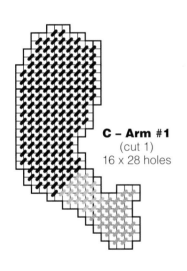

B – Lower Body (cut 1) 45 x 53 holes

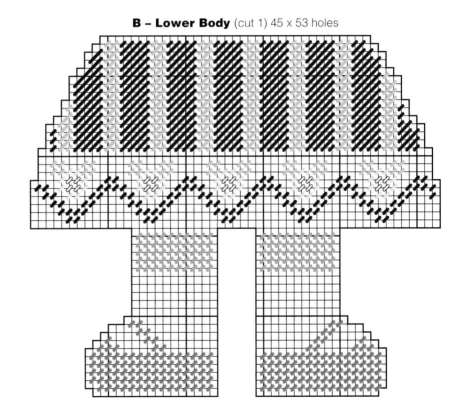

D – Arm #2
(cut 1)
16 x 28 holes

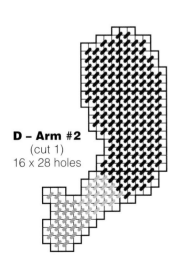

Ready, Set, Stitch!

BASIC INSTRUCTIONS TO GET YOU STARTED

Most plastic canvas stitchers love getting their projects organized before they even step out the door in search of supplies. A few moments of careful planning can make the creation of your project even more fun.

First of all, prepare your work area. You will need a flat surface for cutting and assembly, and you will need a place to store your materials. Good lighting is essential, and a comfortable chair will make your stitching time even more enjoyable.

Do you plan to make one project, or will you be making several of the same item? A materials list appears at the beginning of each pattern. If you plan to make several of the same item, multiply your materials accordingly. Your shopping list is ready.

CANVAS

Most projects can be made using standard-size sheets of canvas. Standard-size sheets of 7-count (7 holes per inch) are always 70 x 90 holes and are about 10½" x 13½". For larger projects, 7-count canvas also comes in 12" x 18" (80 x 120 holes) and 13½" x 22½" (90 x 150 holes) sheets. Other shapes are available in 7-count, including circles, diamonds, purse forms and ovals.

10-count canvas (10 holes per inch) comes only in standard-size sheets, which vary slightly depending on brand. They are 10½" x 13½" (106 x 136 holes) or 11" x 14" (108 x 138 holes).

5-count canvas (5 holes per inch) and 14-count (14 holes per inch) sheets are also available.

Some canvas is soft and pliable, while other canvas is stiffer and more rigid. To prevent canvas from cracking during or after stitching, you'll want to choose pliable canvas for projects that require shaping, like round baskets with curved handles. For easier shaping, warm canvas pieces with a blow-dry hair dryer to soften; dip in cool water to set. If your project is a box or an item that will stand alone, stiffer canvas is more suitable.

Both 7- and 10-count canvas sheets are available in a rainbow of colors. Most designs can be stitched on colored as well as clear canvas. When a pattern does not specify color in the materials list, you can assume clear canvas was used in the photographed model. If you'd like to stitch only a portion of the design, leaving a portion unstitched, use colored canvas to coordinate with yarn colors.

Buy the same brand of canvas for each entire project. Different brands of canvas may differ slightly in the distance between each bar.

MARKING & COUNTING TOOLS

To avoid wasting canvas, careful cutting of each piece is important. For some pieces with square corners, you might be comfortable cutting the canvas without marking it beforehand. But for pieces with lots of angles and cutouts, you may want to mark your canvas before cutting.

Always count before you mark and cut. To count holes on the graphs, look for the bolder lines showing each ten holes. These ten-count lines begin in the lower left-hand corner of each graph and are on the graph to make counting easier. To count holes on the canvas, you may use your tapestry needle, a toothpick or a plastic hair roller pick. Insert the needle or pick slightly in each hole as you count.

Most stitchers have tried a variety of marking tools and have settled on a favorite, which may be crayon, permanent marker, grease pencil or ball point pen. One of the best marking tools is a fine-point overhead projection marker, available at office supply stores. The ink is dark and easy to see and washes off completely with water. After cutting and before stitching, it's important to remove all marks so they won't stain yarn as you stitch or show through stitches later. Cloth and paper toweling removes grease pencil and crayon marks, as do fabric softener sheets that have already been used in your dryer.

SUPPLIES

Yarn, canvas, needles, cutters and most other supplies needed to complete the projects in this book are available at craft and needlework stores and through mail order catalogs. Other supplies are available at fabric, hardware and discount stores. For mail order information, see page 159.

CUTTING TOOLS

You may find it very helpful to have several tools on hand for cutting canvas. When cutting long, straight sections, scissors, craft cutters or kitchen shears are the fastest and easiest to use. For cutting out detailed areas and trimming nubs, you may like using manicure scissors or nail clippers. Many stitchers love using Ultimate Plastic Canvas Cutters, available only from *The Needlecraft Shop* catalog. If you prefer laying your canvas flat when cutting, try a craft knife and cutting surface – self-healing mats designed for sewing and kitchen cutting boards work well.

YARN AND OTHER STITCHING MATERIALS

You may choose two-ply nylon plastic canvas yarn (the color numbers of two popular brands are found in the general materials lists and Color Keys) or four-ply worsted-weight yarn for stitching on 7-count canvas. There are about 42 yards per ounce of plastic canvas yarn and 50 yards per ounce of worsted-weight yarn.

Worsted-weight yarn is widely available and comes in wool, acrylic, cotton and blends. If you decide to use worsted-weight yarn, choose 100% acrylic for best coverage. Select worsted-weight yarn by color instead of the color names or numbers found in the Color Keys. Projects stitched with worsted-weight yarn often "fuzz" after use. "Fuzz" can be removed by shaving it off with a fabric shaver to make your project look new again.

Plastic canvas yarn comes in about 60 colors and is a favorite of many plastic canvas designers. These yarns "wear" well both while stitching and in the finished product. When buying plastic canvas yarn, shop using the color names or numbers found in the Color Keys, or select colors of your choice.

To cover 5-count canvas, use a doubled strand of worsted-weight or plastic canvas yarn.

Choose sport-weight yarn or #3 pearl cotton for stitching on 10-count canvas. To cover 10-count canvas using six-strand embroidery floss, use 12 strands held together. Single and double plies of yarn will also cover 10-count and can be used for embroidery or accent stitching worked over needlepoint stitches – simply separate worsted-weight yarn into 2-ply or plastic canvas yarn into 1-ply. Nylon plastic canvas yarn does not perform as well as knitting worsted when separated and perform as well as knitting worsted when separated and

can be frustrating to use, but it is possible. Just use short lengths, separate into single plies and twist each ply slightly.

Embroidery floss or #5 pearl cotton can also be used for embroidery, and each covers 14-count canvas well.

Metallic cord is a tightly-woven cord that comes in dozens of glittering colors. Some are solid-color metallics, including gold and silver, and some have colors interwoven with gold or silver threads. If your metallic cord has a white core, the core may be removed for super-easy stitching. To do so, cut a length of cord; grasp center core fibers with tweezers or fingertips and pull. Core slips out easily. Though the sparkly look of metallics will add much to your project, you may substitute contrasting colors of yarn.

Natural and synthetic raffia straw will cover 7-count canvas if flattened before stitching. Use short lengths to prevent splitting, and glue ends to prevent unraveling.

CUTTING CANVAS

Follow all Cutting Instructions, Notes and labels above graphs to cut canvas. Each piece is labeled with a letter of the alphabet. Square-sided pieces are cut according to hole count, and some may not have a graph.

Unlike sewing patterns, graphs are not designed to be used as actual patterns but rather as counting, cutting and stitching guides. Therefore, graphs may not be actual size. Count the holes on the graph (see Marking & Counting Tools on page 154), mark your canvas to match, then cut. The old carpenters' adage – "Measure twice, cut once" – is good advice. Trim off the nubs close to the bar, and trim all corners diagonally.

For large projects, as you cut each piece, it is a good idea to label it with its letter and name. Use sticky labels, or fasten scrap paper notes through the canvas with a twist tie or a quick stitch with a scrap of yarn. To stay organized, you many want to store corresponding pieces together in zip-close bags.

If you want to make several of a favorite design to give as gifts or sell at bazaars, make cutting canvas easier and faster by making a master pattern. From colored canvas, cut out one of each piece required. For duplicates, place the colored canvas on top of clear canvas and cut out. If needed, secure the canvas pieces together with paper fasteners, twist ties or yarn. By using this method, you only have to count from the graphs once.

If you accidentally cut or tear a bar or two on your canvas, don't worry! Boo-boos can usually be repaired in one of several ways: heat the tip of a metal skewer and melt the canvas back together; glue torn bars with a tiny drop of craft glue, super glue or hot glue; or reinforce the torn section with a separate piece of canvas placed at the back of your work. When reinforcing with extra canvas, stitch through both thicknesses.

NEEDLES & OTHER STITCHING TOOLS

Blunt-end tapestry needles are used for stitching plastic canvas. Choose a No. 16 needle for stitching 5- and 7-count, a No. 18 for stitching 10-count and a No. 24 for stitching 14-count canvas. A small pair of embroidery scissors for snipping yarn is handy. Try using needle-nosed jewelry pliers for pulling the needle through several thicknesses of canvas and out of tight spots too small for your hand.

STITCHING THE CANVAS

Stitching Instructions for each section are found after the Cutting Instructions. First, refer to the illustrations of basic stitches found on page 157 to familiarize yourself with the stitches used. Illustrations will be found near the graphs for pieces worked using special stitches. Follow the numbers on the tiny graph beside the illustration to make each stitch – bring your needle up from the back of the work on odd numbers and down through the front of the work on the even numbers.

Before beginning, read the Stitching Instructions to get an overview of what you'll be doing. You'll find that some pieces are stitched using colors and stitches indicated on graphs, and for other pieces you will be given a color and stitch to use to cover the entire piece.

Cut yarn lengths between 18" to 36". Thread needle; do not tie a knot in the end. Bring your needle up through the canvas from the back, leaving a short length of yarn on the wrong side of the canvas. As you begin to stitch, work over this short length of yarn. If you are beginning with Continental Stitches, leave a 1" length, but if you are working longer stitches, leave a longer length.

In order for graph colors to contrast well, graph colors may not match yarn colors. For instance, a light yellow may be selected to represent the metallic cord color gold, or a light blue may represent white yarn.

When following a graph showing several colors, you may want to work all the stitches of one color at the same time. Some stitchers prefer to work with several colors at once by threading each on a separate needle and letting the yarn not being used hang on the wrong side of the work. Either way, remember that strands of yarn run across the wrong side of the work may show through the stitches from the front.

As you stitch, try to maintain an even tension on the yarn. Loose stitches will look uneven, and tight stitches will let the canvas show through. If your yarn twists as you work, you may want to let your needle and yarn hang and untwist occasionally.

When you end a section of stitching or finish a thread, weave the yarn through the back side of your last few stitches, then trim it off.

CONSTRUCTION & ASSEMBLY

After all pieces of an item needing assembly are stitched, you will find the order of assembly is listed in the Stitching Instructions and sometimes illustrated in Diagrams found with the graphs. For best results, join pieces in the order written. Refer to the Stitch Key and to the directives near the graphs for precise attachments.

FINISHING TIPS

To combat glue strings when using a hot glue gun, practice a swirling motion as you work. After placing the drop of glue on your work, lift the gun slightly and swirl to break the stream of glue, as if you were making an ice cream cone. Have a cup of water handy when gluing. For those times that you'll need to touch the glue, first dip your finger into the water just enough to dampen it. This will minimize the glue sticking to your finger, and it will cool and set the glue more quickly.

To attach beads, use a bit more glue to form a cup around the bead. If too much shows after drying, use a craft knife to trim off excess glue.

Scotchguard® or other fabric protectors may be used on your finished projects. However, avoid using a permanent marker if you plan to use a fabric protector, and be sure to remove all other markings before stitching. Fabric protectors can cause markings to bleed, staining yarn.

FOR MORE INFORMATION

Sometimes even the most experienced needlecrafters can find themselves having trouble following instructions. If you have difficulty completing your project, write to Plastic Canvas Editors, *The Needlecraft Shop*, 23 Old Pecan Road, Big Sandy, Texas 75755.

Stitch Guide

NEEDLEPOINT STITCHES

CONTINENTAL STITCH

can be used to stitch designs or fill in background areas.

REVERSE CONTINENTAL STITCH

can be used to stitch designs or fill in background areas.

LONG STITCH

is a horizontal or vertical stitch used to stitch designs or fill in background areas. Can be stitched over two or more bars.

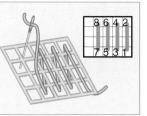

SLANTED GOBELIN STITCH

can be used to stitch designs or fill in background areas. Can be stitched over two or more bars in vertical or horizontal rows.

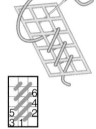

OVERCAST

is used to finish edges. Stitch two or three times in corners for complete coverage.

WHIPSTITCH

is used to join two or more pieces together.

HERRINGBONE WHIPSTITCH

MODIFIED TURKEY WORK STITCH

is used to fill in background areas or as an embroidery stitch to add a loopy or fringed texture. Stitch over one bar leaving a loop, then stitch over the same bar to anchor the loop.

HERRINGBONE OVERCAST

SCOTCH STITCH

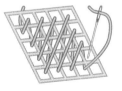

LOOP WHIPSTITCH

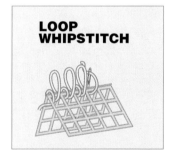

HERRINGBONE STITCH

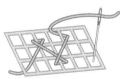

SMYRNA CROSS STITCH

can be used as a needlepoint stitch or as an embroidery stitch stitched over background stitches with contrasting yarn or floss.

MOSAIC STITCH

ALTERNATING SLANTED GOBELIN

SHEAF STITCH

Stitches continued on next page

EMBROIDERY STITCHES

COUCHING STITCH

STRAIGHT STITCH
is usually used as an embroidery stitch to add detail. Stitches can be any length and can go in any direction. Looks like Backstitch except stitches do not touch.

BACKSTITCH
is usually used as an embroidery stitch to outline or add detail. Stitches can be any length and go in any direction.

LARK'S HEAD KNOT

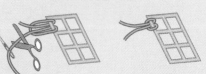

FRENCH KNOT
is usually used as an embroidery stitch to add detail. Can be made in one hole or over a bar. If dot on graph is in hole as shown, come up and go down with needle in same hole.

CROSS STITCH
can be used as a needle-point stitch or as an embroidery stitch stitched over background stitches with contrasting yarn or floss.

CONTINUOUS LARK'S HEAD KNOT

Acknowledgments

We would like to express our appreciation to the many people who helped create this book. Our special thanks go to each of the talented designers who contributed original designs.

Thanks to the following for photography locations and props: John & Leah Darby, Longview, Texas; Craig & Jan Jaynes, Kilgore, Texas; and Joe & Malia McDole and Beau & Patricia Lewis of Tyler, Texas.

Finally, we wish to express our gratitude to the following manufacturers for their generous contribution of materials and supplies:

Ad-Tech™
Princess Glue Gun (low-temp) and oval glue sticks – *Game Time*

Aleene's
Tack It Over & Over repositionable glue – *Fresh Veggies*

Bel-Tree Corporation
Animal eyes – *'Stitches' the Cat*

Darice®
Nylon Plus™ yarn – *Musical Shelf Sitters, Holiday Friends, Door Guard, Tool Time Toys*
Metallic cord – *Twilight Teddy, Purple Passion, Jeweled Snowflakes, Cozy Snowman, Door Guard, Hoedown*
Raffia straw – *Cozy Snowman*
5-count canvas – *Log Cabin Set*
Canvas circles – *Log Cabin Set, April Showers*
Canvas shapes – *Purple Passion*
Colored canvas – *Christmas Joy Tote, Door Guard*
Ultra Stiff™ canvas – *'Stitches' the Cat*

DMC

#3 pearl cotton – *Slim Snowman, Ginger Love, Animal Circus, Basket of Chicks, Santa Basket, Cozy Snowman, Celestial Santa, Little Miss Mirror*
Embroidery floss – *Fresh Veggies, Cookie Chain, 'Stitches' the Cat*

J.&P. Coats / Coats & Clark / Anchor

Embroidery floss – *Victorian Fan*
Red Heart Classic yarn – *Game Time*

Offray

Ribbon – *Homemade Love, Cookie Chain*

Pepperell Braiding Company, Inc.

Rexlace craft lace – *Giraffe Coin Bank*

The Beadery

Acrylic stones – *Jeweled Snowflakes, Holiday Friends*

Toner Plastics

Plastic glow lacing – *Twilight Teddy*

Uniek® Crafts

Needloft® yarn – *Slim Snowman, Homemade Love, Ginger Love, Baby Shower, Animal Circus, Twilight Teddy, April Showers, Mr. & Mrs. Hop, Purple Passion, Basket of Chicks, Star of David, Fresh Veggies, Apples for Teacher, Teacher's Tissues, Halloween Treat Bags, Santa Basket, Cozy Snowman, Cookie Chain, Red Star Bowl, Christmas Joy Tote, Celestial Santa, 'Stitches' the Cat, Crayon Basket, Hoedown, Little Miss Mirror*
Metallic cord – *Mr. & Mrs. Hop, Red Star Bowl*
Colored canvas – *Baby Shower*
Canvas shapes – *Mr. & Mrs. Hop, Jeweled Snowflakes, Red Star Bowl*

Wright's

Gold cord – *Cookie Chain*

For supplies, first shop your local craft and needlework stores. If you are unable to find the supplies you need, write to the address below for a free catalog. The Needlecraft Shop *carries plastic canvas in a variety of shapes, sizes and colors, plastic canvas yarn and a large selection of pattern books.*

23 Old Pecan Road, Big Sandy, Texas 75755
(903) 636-4000 or 1-800-259-4000

Index

Designers